God's Relentless Pursuit

Discovering His Heart
for Humanity

PHIL STROUT
with Jason Chatraw

ampelōn
PUBLISHING

God's Relentless Pursuit
Copyright ©2004 by Phil Strout with Jason Chatraw
Revised and updated edition Copyright ©2014

Requests for information should be address to:
Ampelon Publishing
PO Box 140675
Boise, ID 83714

To order other Ampelon Publishing products, visit us on the web at:
www.AmpelonPublishing.com

ISBN: 0-9748825-1-8

Printed in the United States of America
Cover design by Colby Dees
Cover photo by Iakov Kalinin / © iStockPhoto

Dedication

———————————

*To Janet, Aaron, and Jenna, my wife and two chil-
dren, who have faithfully been on this journey with me
through the last three decades.*

*Many of the stories in this book, the ups and downs of
the adventure, have been lived as a family. We always wanted
to be a family with a focus. It would have been impossible to
write this book, to live this adventure up to this point, without
you three most extraordinary people. A wife who defines the
word flexibility, a son who has wisdom and experience beyond
his years, and a daughter who has a passion for life that is con-
tagious to all. To each of you, I thank you and love you.*

TABLE OF CONTENTS

Acknowledgments

I WOULD LIKE TO THANK the following people who have helped in the development of these thoughts in walking with me as friends and colleagues, as teachers and students, brothers and sisters. To all of these men and women, I say a hearty, "Thank you!" You will never know how much you have added to my life and to the adventure called the Christian walk.

Brother Earl Tygert, my spiritual father and the first man to take me off to the nations at the age of 17.

Tom and Cynthia Weston, who twice uprooted their family to participate in church planting in Brazil and Chile. Through the consistency of friendship and as dedicated servants, they have shown me the reality of the Christian life.

Mark Fields, who has been a colleague in the development of missions in the Vineyard movement. He is a pleasure to work with in missions development, a learned man who challenges me in many ways, and I thank him for his steady guidance in the development of Vineyard missiology.

Craig Simonian, for his contributions in the material of

the "Father's Heart for the Nations" seminar that we developed together, much of which is included in this book.

Roger and Gloria Cunningham, missionaries in Santiago, Chile — true friends and partners in the cause of Christ.

Cristian Gacitua, a son in the faith, a dear friend, a man I admire and will cheer for until.

To all the pastors and partners who make up International Association of Missions (you know who you are), an eternal thank you for your steadfast faithfulness in fleshing out many of the ideas found in this book.

Bob and Penny Fulton, for their graciousness in embracing us when we moved back to the United States and encouraged us to get involved in missions development in the Vineyard movement.

And finally, I want to acknowledge again my wife Janet's consistent help and companionship in living out this great adventure.

Foreword

SOMETIMES WHEN I READ a book, I wonder whether the author actually lives the things he or she writes about, or if they are simply sharing an interesting new theory. With Phil Strout, I do not have that question. I know that he lives the things he writes about. For nearly a decade, we have had the privilege of working together in the development of missions within the Vineyard movement in the United States. Phil's passion and commitment to encouraging others to join with God in His mission has resulted in hundreds of churches being mobilized. These churches now work cross-culturally for the Kingdom in their own neighborhoods and around the world.

Phil has been a missionary, church planter, pastor, and missions mobilizer; always a leader with a desire to involve others. His heart is to "put the cookies on the bottom shelf" where they are accessible to everyone. In *God's Relentless Pursuit*, he makes accessible the truth that theologians describe as the *Missio Dei*, the mission of God. He challenges his readers to discover the truth of a God that is already at work and to join Him in His mission as one of His missional people. I am thrilled that Phil has put into print the substance of what he has taught around the country with such impact.

Mark Fields
VineyardUSA, Director of Missions & Intercultural Ministry
2004

"HEADED FOR THE RHUBARB"

How God pursued me
and started my adventure

AS I ROUNDED THE CORNER on my motorcycle, I locked eyes with the young woman in her station wagon pulling out of a restaurant parking lot. Panicked that she might run over me, she stomped on her brakes, creating an insurmountable roadblock. Had she continued pulling out onto the road and accelerated, all would have been fine — but she didn't, and there was nothing I could do to avoid her.

As I slammed into her station wagon, which was covered by more metal than a Sherman tank, my motorcycle skidded away from me and I landed with my legs positioned just in front of the back tires of her station wagon. Panicked again, the woman put the car in gear and drove forward, oblivious to the fact that I was beneath her car. As she drove over my legs, I screamed in pain, which frightened her yet again. In a misguided effort to assist me and get out of the way, she put the car in reverse and backed over my legs a second time. While I have never claimed to be the sharpest tool in the shed, when she backed over me the second time, I knew I had better not scream for fear that she would drive over me a third time.

Lying on the road, I tried to regain my senses. Just moments before, I was a 16-year-old boy, returning from an errand for my job and enjoying the beautiful 1973 summer in southern Maine. I had given little thought to my purpose in life or my future. Now, everything began to change.

Witnesses to the accident began to crowd around my body, giving me instruction on what to do or what not to do. I remember someone saying, "Don't get up. Don't move. Someone has called the ambulance." But seeing no need to remain on the ground when I felt fine, I got up and dusted off some dirt.

Standing upright, I suddenly realized I had no broken bones, no cuts, no bruises, no lesions, no scratches. Only my motorcycle was slightly scratched with a broken indicator light. Everyone who had quickly gathered around was amazed that I could stand up, much less walk away without any injury. With no reason to stick around, I climbed onto my motorcycle and drove away. As I was leaving the scene of the accident, I remember thinking, "What was that all about?" I had just run into a car, been run over by a car twice, and gotten up and walked away. The issues regarding my life and future, all of a sudden, rushed to the forefront of my mind after what I had just experienced.

Reflecting on that accident years later, I now understand that God was pursuing me. He wanted to reveal Himself to me in a way that prompted me to respond to His call. That accident was no accident. God was trying to reach me, and it was my first experience with the supernatural power of God. But it wasn't the first time I had experienced God's relentless pursuit.

Not long before my motorcycle accident, I came home one night from partying with my friends and I turned on the television. As I stood in front of the TV turning the knob about a dozen times between the four channels we received, I kept skipping past a man, who was dressed in a suit, talking. Finally, I stopped on the channel to see what he was talking about and I remember thinking, "I want to be clean like that man." It wasn't a prayer or even a deep spiritual moment, but I knew I wanted to leave behind the life I was living. (By the way, that man was Billy Graham.)

At that moment, God planted a desire in my heart. Sometime around my motorcycle accident, I attended a Chick Correa concert at a nearby college with some of my buddies. Before the concert, we went out and partied pretty hard, and as show time drew near, I felt extremely ill. I was sick to my stomach — I turned three shades of green and made a mess of myself. While at the concert, I asked my friends to take me to the hospital or take me home. They simply laughed and stayed in the concert, as I went to the car to wait for them to return.

Sitting in that car, I remember thinking that this was a strange way for friends to treat each other — and I was just as guilty as they were. I was just like them. I probably wouldn't have given up my ticket to a Chick Correa concert either. Then I saw it: there we were. We were exposed — and I considered us to be sick people. We treated each other badly and used each other. Reflecting on that night, I see it was an encounter with God as well. He revealed my own need, my own sin nature, and uncovered what was really in my heart.

A few months later, I was sitting on a bridge in a little town in Maine, watching the river go beneath the bridge. As I watched the river go down stream, my 16-year-old mind started churning. I thought about how only the strong fish can swim back against the current, spawn, and leave life behind. I wondered what I was going to leave behind. It was a sobering moment.

At one point, these fish are born and then have to come back up stream. I realized that they had to go full circle. I was thinking, "I wonder if I will live the full circle of life." Again, that was the fourth encounter I had regarding issues in my life. It was an encounter with God where I understood how I wanted to fulfill my purpose in life. Before that moment, I had never given it a thought.

Just as I was lost in thought, I looked down the bridge

and there was a group of young people from a local church strolling along. They were kids I had known since kindergarten, practically my entire life — and I simply didn't know they were Christians. As John Wimber, the father of the Vineyard movement, used to say, "If they were Christians, they had never blown their cover." They stopped and invited me to one of their meetings. When I got to the meeting, I was taken aback by the content of the meeting. They were singing songs about Jesus. The only time I had heard His name was within the context of swearing. Their songs and talk intrigued me, but I didn't understand the whole meaning of it. I was not convinced yet that anything in my life needed to change.

Then on February 11, 1974, I was hanging out in the hallway at my high school when a pretty young girl approached us and asked us if we would be interested in attending a meeting to hear a missionary from Japan and a young man from Brazil speak. I didn't know much about missionaries or what she was talking about, but I figured since she was cute, I ought to go to the meeting. And so did my buddies. To this day, I don't know why I responded in a positive manner.

At the meeting, a group of teenagers sang about Jesus, which was still baffling to me. There was an elderly gentleman sitting on the floor with his legs crossed. He invited us to pray and then loudly said, "Oh, sweet, Jesus!" My first thought was one of pity: "That poor old man thinks somebody is listening to him." I thought maybe senility had begun to settle over him. Then a 25-year-old Brazilian man began to share about life in his country. He spoke broken English and plowed on without the assistance of a translator. But he spoke enough English that I understood him. As he talked about how he had delved into the drug and alcohol scene, I was with him. Then he said this phrase, "Then I met the Lord!" That's where my cables could not connect.

I had no idea what he was talking about. He kept talking about accepting Christ and coming to know God. But I still didn't understand. Yet, as he was speaking a thought kept racing through my head: "This is the truth. Buy it and never let it go." Even though I attended church at Christmas and Easter, I had never read the Bible — but I suddenly had the sense that what they were talking about was the truth.

As the meeting came to a close, the elderly man gave what I now know to be an invitation to receive Christ. He said, "If any of you wants to know God, raise your hand." I thought to myself, "If God is real, who wouldn't want to know Him?" So, I raised my hand. Then the elderly man said, "All of you who raised your hand, I want you to come join me in the kitchen."

"Oh, no!" I thought. "If God is real, He is right here in the living room." A few kids went into the kitchen, but then the man said, "We know there's someone else here, so please join us in the kitchen whenever you're ready." And I knew that they knew that I was the one kid not going into the kitchen who wanted to find out more. So, I simply dug my fingers into the side of the chair I was sitting in and decided not to go into the kitchen. I knew it was bait-and-switch. Being a Maine yankee, I was stubborn and wasn't about to move.

As the rest of the group broke for Kool-Aid and cookies, the pretty little girl who invited me looked at me and said, "Well, Phil, what did you think?" And I thought, "If this is true, this is the best deal in town." But she was cute, so I was trying to play it cool. I didn't have a legitimate argument for her as to why it wasn't the best deal in town, but I didn't want to let her know that I was buying into it. So, I decided to ask her a few questions.

I shot back with a question: "If God is real, why are there so many starving children in Africa?" The truth of the matter is that I never had thought of the starving children in Africa before in my life. For that question and many more, this girl opened what seemed to be a 40-pound Thompson Chain Reference Bible and found an answer. I was amazed that she always found an answer to my question in the Bible. After several questions, I began to wonder if she helped write the book!

While I was sitting in bewilderment at this girl's knowledge of the Bible, my friends were restless. "Hey, we're getting out of here. Are you coming?" they asked. As I stood up to join them and tell this girl good-bye, she looked deep into my eyes and firmly said while pointing at me, "You don't really want to leave." I wasn't used to being told what to do by a young lady, but she was right. She had read my mail — I didn't want to leave. My friends began chuckling and muttering about how I was going to get religious.

So, I turned around and said to her, "You know, you're right. I don't want to leave." We sat back down and she answered a few more questions. Then I told her maybe I should go home and think about it and then deal with God tomorrow. Immediately, she showed me another verse about today being the day of salvation. She stopped me dead in my tracks with one final question: "What if you die tonight?" I thought, "Wouldn't that be like me to miss eternity by eight hours?" So, after some discussion, I said, "I want to do this." With her eyes opening wide and an insecure expression on her face, she said, "You do?" But she didn't know what to do next. She then took me over to the older gentleman and told him that I wanted to receive Christ.

The elderly gentleman asked me, "What do you know about God?"

"Nothing," I said.

Then he said, "What do you know about the Bible?"

I said again, "Nothing."

"Good," he said and took me into a side room. Then he said, "Now, tell God what you want."

So, I prayed a prayer like this, "If this is true and if you are real, then this is the best deal in town — and I want in." About five minutes later when I came out of the room, I had no idea that all the people in the meeting knew what I was doing while I was in the other room. Everyone began approaching me, shaking my hand and congratulating me. It was totally uncomfortable. And as we were milling around, the older gentleman, whom I came to know as Brother Earl, came up to me and said, "Tell everyone what just happened to you." And I said, "Jesus just accepted me!" I didn't know what to say. Then he asked me, "How would you like to go with me to Brazil this summer and tell the young people there what happened to you?" I said, "What do you mean? What happened to me?" He said, "You know, that Jesus just became your Lord and Savior and that you get a brand new start. I want you to tell the young people about what Jesus has done for you." I didn't even pray about it. Just over four months later, I found myself on an evangelistic team in Brazil sharing the Gospel as a 17-year-old.

That was the start of my journey with God. I was not on a quest to find God. I was not searching for God. I was not even a church attender. No one had really been sharing Christ with me. But now I realize those four encounters were the wooings of God — God's relentless pursuit of me. A desire had been planted in my heart. In each of those significant incidents in my life, God was working both openly and behind the scenes to draw me to Him. And He used normal, everyday people to show me what a life with Him was all about.

God planted in me a seed of desire to get more out of life. He intersected with my life supernaturally. He revealed the sinful nature of my heart. He showed me that my life could be filled with purpose. At the time, I couldn't see it, but now I realize how God was orchestrating events and relationships in my life to draw me unto Him. God was actively, relentlessly pursuing my heart.

In Maine, we have a saying we use when we want to express that we're headed for an unknown adventure: "Hold on, Martha, we're headed for the rhubarb." And when I launched out on my adventure with God over 30 years ago, I had no idea where I was headed, but I knew I wanted to go with Him.

I like to say I was out among the stop signs of life — normal, everyday life — and God came after me. This book is about how relentless God is as He pursues the hearts of men and women, boys and girls. This is about the mission that God is on. This is about ordinary people who have been pursued by an awesome God. If you are a stay-at-home mom, a stockbroker, a farmer, a truck driver, a teacher, a coach, or a carpenter, this book is for you.

I want to show you how each day you will run into God's plans and purposes for those around you — and how you can be a part of changing their lives forever by obeying the leading of the Holy Spirit. I want to show you that God is at work all the time, everywhere in your everyday life, in and among the stop signs of your life. It is my hope that, as this book unfolds, you will see how you were pursued by God and how you may interact with Him as a vessel to help other people meet Him.

So, hold on, Martha, we're headed for the rhubarb!

Chapter One

MISSIONAL GOD

Discovering His intent for us

---

*Love, which is the essence of God, is not
for levity, but for the total worth of man.*
— Ralph Waldo Emerson

IF ONLY YOU COULD you could have seen it, the most beautiful sand castle in the world. At least to eight-year-old Thomas and his five-year-old sister Jennifer, it was the most beautiful sand castle they had ever seen. One perfect sunny day on the sandy white beaches of the Gulf of Mexico, they poured their little hearts and souls into creating a castle that would rival Neuschwanstein. Every little detail, down to the window sills and designs above the door — Thomas and Jennifer thought of everything. Well, almost everything.

The serene waves that lapped the shore eventually consumed the siblings' castle like a vengeful storm. As the last trickle of foam drifted backward over the castle and awaited the next incoming wave, the damage was unimaginable. One wing of the fortress was completely gone, another just half of a blob. The form and detail that once distinguished Thomas and Jennifer's castle from all the others on the beach had vanished. Both stared at the devastation with mouths agape. It was only a matter of seconds before another wave came fast and furious, doubling the damage to their creation.

Little Jennifer scrunched up her face and opened her mouth, wailing aloud as tears began streaming down both sides of her face. Her dreams of playing with her dolls in this fanciful little world were gone. Young Thomas just stared with a blank expression as another wave washed over the castle. Unable to bear it anymore, Jennifer turned her back on the tide and raced toward her mother, explaining what happened between broken sobs. Yet, the sympathetic ear of her mother was not enough to stop her crying.

Thomas marched toward their family's beach area, determined to address the situation. He tenderly put his arm around Jennifer and said, "It's OK, Jennifer. We can rebuild our castle — and we'll make it just like before." Suddenly, Jennifer stopped crying and wiped her nose with the back of her hand. "Really?" she asked. "Yeah," said Thomas, "and we'll do it together."

God's Great Intention

Have you ever watched something you created with such care and precision vanish before your eyes? It may have been a physical object. It may have been a relationship. It may have been your career. But in an instant, it's gone — and we think whatever it is we lost, we may never see it again.

You're not alone. In fact, God experienced just such great loss years ago in the Garden of Eden. He spent six days breathing life into the world — and creating mankind to share it with Him. And then in an instant, that relationship with mankind was severed, broken, damaged.

In Genesis 1 and 2, we have the whole picture of what God

truly intended for life on earth to be like. We see paradise and the idea of community. We see the thought of there being community in relationship with God, not just one man or one family. We see God walking with these people and being intimate, plus we have the description of Paradise. This is at the beginning of the story because this is what God intended for us to have.

If we could stop at Genesis 1 and 2, this would have been awesome. Unfortunately, that's not how this story unfolded.

Instead, what we have is the fall of man, which can sound so sterile in those terms. There was an evil outside of man, which tempted Eve who tempted Adam — and they fell. Their whole identity had been wrapped up in God, and then when they stepped away from God, they understood that they were naked. Sin entered the world. Shame was introduced. Pain became a part of life; separation made itself known. I don't think we have the capacity to understand the depth, breadth, and width of the fall of man. It wasn't just a stumble out of grace, but an exit from paradise.

Throughout my years as a pastor, people have oftentimes asked me, "Where is this good God when bad things happen?" Or "How can a God of love let these things happen?" It's not that God has gone anywhere; it's just that now there is pervasive sin in the world as a result of the fall. We need to understand the depth and long-term effect that happened in that split second when Adam took his identity away from God and put it upon himself. It's painful, and the long-term effect has been the entrance and existence of sin in the world.

But God refused to give up at that point. He didn't let it go. I've thought many times if I were God and the fall happened, I would've started over — and who would've been around to know it? I would've called it a mulligan and started afresh. But that's not what God did. He was determined to rebuild His masterful creation just like He originally set out to do; just like little Thomas decided to do. We must realize the fact that God really loves us and received great pleasure in not only creating the crown jewel, but also in relating to the crown jewel — mankind. God began His relentless pursuit of humanity.

Creator God

Whenever I'm sitting in the pew and a pastor says, "Let's open our Bibles to Genesis 1," I get nervous. At best, I figure I'm in for a long sermon. However, I can promise you that even though we are beginning with some verses in Genesis 1, by the time you finish this chapter, you will have the story of the entire Bible.

Traditionally, we learn the story of the creation process with a focus on what was being created. On the first day, God created the light. Then the second day, God created the heavens and the waters. On the third day, He created dry land with plants and trees. And so the story goes. Yet, while we focus on what was being created, we miss who was creating everything.

In Genesis 1 and 2, Elohim—Creator God—is mentioned 35 times.

"In the beginning God ..." (vs. 1)
"Then God said ..." (vs. 3)
"God saw ..." (vs.4)
"God called ..." (vs. 5)
"Then God said ..." (vs. 6)

As we study these first two chapters of Genesis, we realize God is the one who is doing everything. This is all about Him. It's about God creating and about Him being pleased with what He is creating. He is an omnipotent God, so powerful that we struggle to fathom the ease with which He created everything around us.[1]

In Genesis 1:16, we read almost a footnote to God's creation, but it cannot be dismissed so easily: "He made the stars also." There are scientists who spend their whole lives studying one star. There are teams of scientists who spend their entire lives concentrating on just one galaxy. For all their work, scientists tell us that the distance from one end of the Milky Way to the other is 100,000 light years and that this galaxy contains over two billion stars. The nearby Andromeda galaxy is 2.2 million light years away, roughly 11,700,000,000,000,000,000 miles away! Yet when we read about God's creation of the stars in the Bible, it is five words long — "He made the stars also." God looked at the expanse of the heavens and wanted to create something magnificent to fill the void. Yet, in Scripture it almost reads as if He were throwing pepperoni on a pizza! While the things God created are truly amazing, we must realize that God was the One creating them.

The Crown Jewel

The whole story of creator God culminates in His creation of Adam and Eve. When He finished after six days, God observed that "it was very good" (Genesis 1:31). God analyzed the human race and looked at Adam. Adam and Eve were the crown jewels of that creation. They not only were good, but they were "very good." It is important to understand that there is a relationship here, a pleasure here. I don't know that we understand what all was behind "it was very good," but creating Adam brought great pleasure to God's heart.

In Genesis 1, the attention is on Elohim's activity in heaven and earth. But then in Genesis 2:7, the attention shifts to God's interaction with mankind. This is where Elohim-Adonai breathes life into His creation. The spotlight begins to shift to the first couple who can be seen walking hand in hand with God.

God was powerful as creator God, but also intimate in forming and breathing life, as well as walking and having fellowship with Adam and Eve. Looking at the creation with the emphasis on the creator God, we recognize the majesty of a powerful, yet near and intimate God. That's what we want to see. Looking at the creation scene helps us see not only His majesty but also His desire for intimacy with us.

Community, Intimacy & Paradise in the Garden

Community and intimacy are cornerstones of life with God — and those truths were immediately revealed through the depiction of Adam and Eve's life with God in the Garden of

Eden. As we study life in the garden, some elements come to light. Early in the Scripture, we see the idea of community being presented to us. There is God spending time in relationship with Adam and Eve. God asks them to take it one step further with the command to "be fruitful and multiply." At the essence of God's heart is community, which we see immediately in the way that He set up the Garden to exist.

In my journey, community has always been crucial for me and my family. When I first started this adventure, I had no idea what I was getting into. My first impression was that it was about my sins being forgiven and getting into heaven. Then I began to realize it was about people. It wasn't just me and God, but me and God and a bunch of other people. Those first few months after God tracked me down were so crucial. As I gathered night after night at the Sawyer house with other young people in my town who had also been arrested by God, we would dive into the scripture. I realized how important it was to be connected with those people. It became a very important part of my Christianity.

In the late 1970s as I was growing in my walk with God, we had a Bible study that met as an extra-curricular meeting in our church. This wasn't part of a small group program in a church; just a group of people who were so hungry for God's Word that we just met. We would eat together, worship together, and then play a tape of some preacher because there was no Bible teacher among us. Then we would discuss the tape's topic for another hour or two, praying for each other.

The kids were sacked out across the floor as these small group meetings would last four or five hours. From that experience together, we developed the richest relationships, some of which have lasted over 30 years for me and my wife. I look back and see that this was intended in the garden. God knew that this human life was to be carried out together.

As true community develops, so does intimacy. Adam and Eve didn't just know who God was; they spent time sharing their hearts with Him. They were intimate with God. So often, we struggle to connect intimately with God, but God's heart is for us to know Him as deeply as possible. In the Garden, intimacy was easy to achieve, as Adam and Eve discovered.

Because of the depth of community and genuine intimacy, paradise was the natural outcome of where Adam and Eve lived. Today, it is difficult to find deep community that is self-less in nature, much less find intimacy with others. Most people feel quite comfortable wearing masks to hide what is really in their hearts. But not in the Garden. There was no shame, no pain, no death, no crying. There was no cancer, no HIV, no heart disease. When God summarized His creation on the sixth day by saying, "That is very good," we see the heart of the Lord. I believe what we see is the pleasure that God had in what He created, culminating in the crown jewel, which is mankind. God delighted in what occurred in Genesis 1 and 2.

But there is a Genesis 3—and this is the point at which sin makes its way onto the scene—and it's also the point when God pronounces judgment on the serpent and declares His plan.

God's Mission

In His infinite love for us, God emphatically states His mission after sin entered the world. Suddenly, there was something standing squarely between Him and relationship with Adam and Eve. Sin was now poisoning paradise, but God did not lose hope that His paradise could be restored. So, He laid out His plan to correct what had gone awry.

> *And I will put enmity between you and the woman, and between your seed and her seed; he shall bruise you on the head, and you shall bruise him on the heel.* — Genesis 3:15

This is where God makes His will known. He steps up to the plate and says, "I will solve this problem." He didn't look for Adam and Eve to find a solution for this grave dilemma. He says, "I *can* solve this problem, and I *will* solve this problem." And in one verse, God introduces the mission that He begins. This is the decisive factor and the launching pad of God coming forward and saying, "I'm going to save you." This is God taking the initiative. This is a paradigm of understanding mission.

As we look closely at this passage, we realize it was not man who took the initiative — it was God. God proclaimed that He would cause the enmity between the serpent and the seed of the woman. God openly prophesied the coming of Christ, the key to restoration in the world.

After the fall of man, God throws down the gauntlet and decides to go after the human race. He's not asking the human race to solve the problem; He knew that would be impossible. It was God who saw what happened and began the journey to win us back. He did this to the point that the rest of the Bible is the unfolding drama of how He carries out Genesis 3:15.

Back to the Future

Are you interested in whether God succeeded at His plan? As we peer into the end of God's story of redemption of mankind, we discover the outcome in Revelation 21 and 22. On the Isle of Patmos, a small island just off the coast of present-day Turkey, is an exiled John the apostle. And John receives a revelation of what the new heaven and new earth look like.

> *Then I saw a new heaven and a new earth; for the first heaven and the first earth passed away, and there is no longer any sea. And I saw the holy city, new Jerusalem, coming down out of heaven from God, made ready as a bride adorned for her husband. And I heard a loud voice from the throne, saying, "Behold, the tabernacle of God is among men, and He will dwell among them, and they will be His people, and God Himself will be among them, and He will wipe every tear from their eyes; and there will no longer be any death; there will no longer be any*

mourning or crying or pain; the first things have passed away. — Revelation 21:1-4

And there was more.

Then he showed me a river of the water of life, clear as crystal, coming from the throne of God and of the Lamb, in the middle of its street. On either side of the river was the tree of life, bearing twelve kinds of fruit, yielding its fruit every month; and the leaves of the tree were for the healing of the nations. There will no longer be any curse; and the throne of God and of the Lamb will be in it, and His bond-servants will serve Him; they will see His face, and His name will be on their foreheads. And there will no longer be any night; and they will not have need of the light of a lamp nor the light of the sun, because the Lord God will illumine them; and they will reign forever and ever. — Revelation 22:1-5

Now, this sounds extremely familiar. God is revealing to John the same picture of what He intended for the Garden to be like. You have paradise. You have community. You have intimacy. That's how the room is adorned for the bride and groom. As you read through those passages, you realize there are no tears, no pain, no death. You have God taking us back to the future.

If you take the first two chapters of Genesis and hold it in one hand, those chapters are God's intention in its seed form. And then, if you grab Revelation 21 and 22 with your other hand, you have what John the Apostle sees. He sees the new heaven, the new earth, the new Jerusalem. He sees paradise, community, intimacy. There's no pain, no death, no tears. In one hand you have what God created and lost. And then in the other hand, you have what He got back, not only for Himself but also for us. Between Genesis 1 and 2 and Revelation 21 and 22 is the unfolding drama of how God fulfilled His promise in Genesis 3:15, how He gets us back to the future, how God wins back what was lost. So, here's the story — He creates this awesome paradise with humanity as the crown jewel. Intimacy, community, and paradise are at the thriving heart of this. Then comes evil. Evil poisons the whole thing, and the relationship is severed. And it was only God who could put this thing back together.

God's Desire

God has not left us on the shores to be ravaged by the waves of sin. He didn't walk away and leave us with no way to reach Him. As we embark on our journey of life, we should understand that it is not about how we conquer the elements and find our way home on our own — it is about how He embarks on a journey to find us, to chase us down, and welcome us back into His arms. It's about how He finds us, how God takes us to the place He intended for us to be all along: in the Garden, experiencing true community and intimacy with Him.

I know I was not out searching for God in 1973. Those four God encounters I had before I ever encountered Jesus, I recognize as the wooing of God. That night when I stopped the channel on Billy Graham, a thought came into my head that I wanted to be clean. A car ran over me and I was unharmed. I became sick in the flesh but realized how sick I was in my heart. I reflected on my life and thought about the purpose of my life on earth and my future. All of those experiences helped get me to the place where I realized that I would never understand my life until I was walking with the One who created it. I had no idea that this journey would take me around the globe to live in other countries, learn other cultures, and speak another language. I had no idea when God came wooing me that He would give me family and friends from continents around the globe. I wasn't searching for these things. I wasn't searching for a clean conscience. I didn't know it was an issue. I wasn't searching for community. I wasn't searching for forgiveness. God was relentlessly pursuing my heart. And when God turns a light on in our hearts, He does it because He is committed to come get us.

As we discover God's true heart for us, we quickly realize God is the star of the show. He is the one who created us. We stepped away. We sinned. We fell. And He immediately came after us, not letting us twist in the wind or fall subject to an irreversible fate. He threw down the gauntlet. He said

He would (Genesis 3:15). He pursued us. In the end, we see very clearly how we can return to what we once had. What we see is how He created us and what he intended us to be. The Bible is a commentary on how God actually does this.

God created something wonderful and He really loved it. When it was lost, God took the initiative to get it back. At the end of the Word of God, we see how God won it back. And history is how people have lived it out. It's how we go on toward His return.

God is the hero of this story — not people, not churches, not missionaries, not mission agencies. Since the beginning of time, God has been the one involved in making this mission a reality, not us. As God wins each of our hearts back and we discover the portion of community and intimacy that He has for us today, we become His people. However, when we become His people, we are invited to participate in His mission, His pursuit of the hearts of humanity. When God grips our hearts with His love and compassion, it is unavoidable — and we, too, become missional people.

NOTES

1. Simonian, Craig & Phil Strout. Seminar material entitled, "Father's Heart for the Nations."

Chapter Two

BEING A MISSIONAL PERSON

Embracing the
heart of God

Passion impels our deeds; ideology
supplies the explanations.
— Mason Cooley

WEEPING TEARS OVER HER husband's death, Ruth had watched her life take a cruel and wicked turn — or so it would seem. After marrying into a family from Judah, she became attached to her husband's way of life. She left behind her life as a Moabite. Somehow, her heart had been gripped by one of Naomi's sons, and Ruth made a loyal marital commitment. Yet, when Ruth's husband died, she wanted no part in returning to her old way of life.

When Naomi, Ruth's widowed mother-in-law, prepared to return to freshly prospering Judah, there was a hesitation in bringing Ruth along with her. Naomi had already been through the pain of leaving her own homeland and did not want to have a part in ripping Ruth from her roots. However, Ruth had released her roots long ago when she married.

Incited by both the desperation and freedom that come with nothing to lose, Ruth refused to back down from her desire to follow Naomi back to Judah. "But Ruth said, 'Do not urge me to leave you or turn back from following you; for where you go, I will go, and where you lodge, I will lodge. Your people shall be my people, and your God, my

God. Where you die, I will die, and there I will be buried. Thus may the Lord do to me, and worse, if anything but death parts you and me.' When she saw that she was determined to go with her, she said no more to her" (Ruth 1:16-18).

Ruth shoved aside her past and embraced her future — a future she knew only because of her connection to her husband. Her refusal to go back to her old way of life demonstrated that Ruth saw her place in her new family as lasting, not temporary. Not even death deterred Ruth. Wherever Naomi went, whatever Naomi did — Ruth was going to be there with her, doing it with her.

What's Yours Is Mine

People who truly walk with God embrace what He says and do what He calls them to do. Instead of viewing them as good suggestions, the causes of God become the causes of God's people. And godly people take up such causes with vigor and valor.

In trying to determine how each individual's personality is formed, psychologists and sociologists have dozens of theories. They state factors such as environment, education, and social standing play major roles in developing the personalities of children. And while all those factors contribute to an individual's personal interests and behavioral pattern, not many factors are overtly obvious like that of a child's parent. Whether it's oversaturation or sheer delight in the experience, young children tend to gravitate toward what their parents like.

One of my friends, who is a pastor and father of eight children, shares a similar interest with me: racing. Neither one of us would probably be labeled the stereotypical NASCAR fan, but we both enjoy the sport with a passion. And when you watch my friend's children, I know he isn't just trying to make small talk with me — he really enjoys racing. Not only do his children know NASCAR drivers' names and car numbers as if they were close kin, they all will also stop and stare at the latest and greatest sports car that passes, almost as a sign of respect for the automobile. It is quite evident that the hobbies and passions of the father have been passed down to his children.

God's desire is to pass His passion and zeal for certain areas of life to His people. And we must embrace these things. Early in Genesis after the fall of mankind, we begin to see how God lays out this plan along with His intention of using us to accomplish it. If Genesis 3:15 was the intention of God's plan, Genesis 12:1-3 becomes God's execution of that plan, laid out for the world to see.

> *Now the Lord said to Abram, "Go forth from your country, and from your relatives and from your father's house, to the land which I will show you; and I will make you a great nation, and I will bless you, and make your*

name great; and so you shall be a blessing; and
I will bless those who bless you, and the one who
curses you I will curse. And in you all the fam-
ilies of the earth shall be blessed." — Genesis
12:1-3

With Abram's obedience to God's call on his life, God's
plan of redemption for mankind is set into motion. God sets
the stage with Genesis 3:15, and by His covenant with
Abram, God reaches into the sea of humanity and plucks out
one man. Why Abram? He could have used anyone; but in
His sovereignty, God chose Abram to begin this process,
promising to Abram that He would make him the father of
a great nation.

Many missiologists have referred to God's promise as one
with a "top line" — *I am going to bless you* — and a "bottom
line" — *in order to make you a blessing.* Once God makes this
covenant with Abram, God fulfills His promise, making
Abram the father of a great nation, Israel. And this great nation becomes the people of God.

'Your people shall be my people, and your
God, my God." — Ruth 1:16

In God's magnificence, He makes a great nation from

Abram's seed. Israel is made up of 12 tribes. And out of those 12 tribes, there's one tribe in particular that God carefully uses in His plan of redemption: Judah. As we follow the lineage of the tribe of Judah throughout scripture, we see it is composed of familiar names. And out of one that one tribe comes Jesus. We can follow it through the Old Testament — Abram, Israel, a tribe, a family, a Savior.

In Matthew 1, we can take a cursory glance at Christ's genealogy, tracing it back to Abram. Through those often neglected verses of one man "begetting" another man, we unearth precious jewels, discovering how God used ordinary men and women. He sometimes used the hopeless of society, such as the prostitute Rahab, or an outsider, such as Ruth. Each person played a part in executing His redemptive plan. Nobody earned the "right" to be a part of God's plan. They simply responded when He came to them with an invitation to participate. They began following God and caught His zeal and His passion. They accepted an invitation to join in His mission.

God's Invitation

The moment we make the decision to follow God and forsake our old sinful ways, He extends to us an invitation. After having been part of the objective of His plan, we are now invited to become agents in executing God's plan. It's what being missional people is all about. Through studying scripture and seeing God at work around us, it's clear that He chose to use people to reach people.

Suddenly, God's "top line, bottom line" objective for us becomes clear as well. He blesses us so that we may bless others. He loves us so that we may love others. He reaches us so that we may reach others. As John Wimber, the founder of the Vineyard movement, often said, "We get to give." What we receive from God is designed to be given away.

What we may dismiss as a random selection from the sea of humanity, we find is not random at all. We begin to realize that God is much more intentional about reaching the human heart than we give Him credit for. The drive that was in Ruth's heart to follow Naomi back to her homeland and remain with her was not a coincidence. Instead, Ruth was walking into the very plan God set up for her long ago. Among other things, God demonstrates the inclusive nature of His love. He uses a Moabite in the lineage of His Son, clearly adding to the prophesied lineage of the tribe of Judah. Ruth was an outsider, yet God chose her. Now Ruth became an intrinsic portion of the plan, accepting God's invitation.

In scripture, God issued an invitation to the entire nation of Israel, an invitation to not only become missional people but to walk with a missional God.

> *I am the Lord, I have called you in righteousness, I will also hold you by the hand and watch over you, and I will appoint you as a covenant to the people, as a light to the nations.*
> — Isaiah 42:6

> *He says, "It is too small a thing that You should be My Servant to raise up the tribes of Jacob and to restore the preserved ones of Israel; I will also make You a light of the nations so that My salvation may reach to the end of the earth."* — Isaiah 49:6

The people of Israel are God's people, and His mission becomes their mission. Israel was chosen out of the sovereign purposes of God, not because they were better than others, but to fulfill His purposes. It was for the benefit of people everywhere.

God chose them not because there was something already special about them, but so they could draw others to Him. The blessing of God for Israel was for them to carry out the very purposes that He began in Genesis 3:15.

When talking about what God is doing in our lives and what the purpose of our life is, we have to remember that we are on a mission with God. He's on a mission; therefore, as His people, we are on His mission. He is our God and He is a missional God; therefore, we are missional people.

In Psalms and other Old Testament books, we realize that God's entire plan of redemption isn't just about God's people — it's about all people.

> *God be gracious to us and bless us, and cause His face to shine upon us. That Your way may be known on the earth, Your salvation among all nations.* — Psalm 67:1-2

Even the psalmist was getting it: God's desire is — and always has been — to draw all people to Himself. And early in the history of the world, we see that God gives this mission to the people of Israel. Although Israel did not always understand its purpose while living out the "top line, bottom line" promise made to Abram, the faithful people of Israel played a tremendous role in God's mission to redeem the heart of men and women all over the world throughout time.

Missional People Meet the Messiah

Have you ever lived in high expectancy of future events? I remember, as a child growing up in Maine, the high expectancy I had during the months of April and May for the summer. As nature was beginning to thaw out, I couldn't wait for the summertime. Each passing day, my hopes grew higher. And then when my dad told me we were going to Fenway Park to watch the Red Sox play (Yankees fans, stay with me), there was an enormous longing and expectancy in my heart for the anticipated date circled on the calendar.

Living in the 21st century and reading about the introduction of Jesus into the Jewish culture, we are somewhat cheated. We know and understand (to some extent) the nature of God's plan to redeem the heart of mankind. Jesus' death and resurrection — though powerful and gripping 2,000 years later — is somewhat removed from the world in which we live in today. We struggle to relate what it must have been like to be anxiously awaiting the arrival of the Messiah. But to the people who were walking around the streets of Jerusalem, the Messiah's arrival was the realization of a promise and the beginning of a new mission.

> And there was a man in Jerusalem whose name was Simeon; and this man was righteous and devout, looking for the consolation of Israel; and the Holy Spirit was upon him. And it had been revealed to him by the Holy Spirit that he would not see death before he had seen the Lords Christ. And he came in the Spirit into the temple; and when the parents brought in the child Jesus, to carry out for Him the custom of the law, then he took Him into his arms, and blessed God, and said, "Now Lord, You are releasing Your bond-servant to depart in peace, according to Your word; for my eyes have seen Your salvation, which You have prepared in the presence of all peoples, A LIGHT OF REVELATION TO THE GENTILES, and the glory of Your people Israel." — Luke 2:25-32

This passage ranks as one of my favorites on insight into how God began working out His plan. Though we are missional people, we are on God's mission, not our own. It is God who is relentlessly pursuing our hearts. Adam couldn't rescue himself. Abraham didn't go seeking God. Israel wasn't even a nation. But God made everything happen. We see God's intentions made clear in Genesis 3:15, and then we come to the New Testament and see the pieces begin to fall into place.

> *And there was a man in Jerusalem whose name was Simeon; and this man was righteous and devout, looking for the consolation of Israel; and the Holy Spirit was upon him.* — Luke 2:25

Here, we see Simeon had a visitation from the Holy Spirit, much like John's visitation while on the Isle of Patmos. This was not something Simeon read or learned. God broke into the scene of Simeon's life. The Holy Spirit clearly revealed Himself to Simeon, explaining that he would not die until he had seen the Messiah. So, there Simeon was in the temple, listening to the Holy Spirit, and he saw a family walk through the doors. Joseph and Mary brought this little Jewish baby boy to be circumcised. Thousands of families had brought their children to the temple for the same ritual for which they were bringing Jesus. Simeon had probably seen thousands of little babies go by him and heard the Holy Spirit say, "Nope, not that one." Or, he watched them go by with no witness whatsoever.

But along came this little baby Jesus, and the Holy Spirit arrested Simeon. He took Jesus in his arms, knowing that this was the Messiah by listening to the Holy Spirit. Simeon held the child and said, "For my eyes have seen Your salvation" (vs. 33). He went on to quote Isaiah 49:6: This is the Messiah for all people. This is God on His mission. We have come from Abraham, Israel, the tribe, the family and now the Christ.

Simeon was used in a very sovereign way to say that his eyes had seen the salvation. He testified to this. After seeing thousands of babies, he knew now he had seen *the* one.

As we closely study about the people of God, we see Jesus ministering, raising up a troop of men and women from Israel to take God's message to the world. These people begin hearing Jesus' teachings, and He draws them in and woos them into not only intimacy and relationship with Him but also to His purpose. During the scene at the end of Jesus' life, their destiny is revealed in a clear way: "As the Father has sent Me, I also send you" (John 20:21). Jesus challenges the people to do God's bidding, helping them realize that being God's people means that they also do as God does.

Through the years, I've attended many pastors' conferences and heard this question, "What do you think the Lord is up to?" I've always thought that it was a foolish question, as if God is fickle and changing His mind on a regular basis. It's an innocent question, but I believe it reflects the boredom in our church culture where we're always looking for the latest and the greatest. God is up to the same thing He has always been up to since the fall of mankind.

God was drawing these men and women to be His people — and to become His people, they must take on His very purpose. These disciples are called to do His bidding. He was not only drawing them into intimacy, but He was drawing them into mission: His mission. When we come to the birth of the church at Pentecost, we find a group of people in the upper room who had followed Jesus; now they are dealing with disappointment and disillusionment. They had been instructed to wait for the Spirit from on high. So, they are waiting on Him and worshipping God. As the book of Acts records, these people were baptized by the Holy Spirit at what has commonly been called the birth of the church. This is the continuation of God drawing people to Himself for intimacy which brings community and is carried forth in mission. Without mission, it's hard to talk about the church. God called the church into existence, and these people, led by the apostles, became His testimony on the earth.

Modeling the Mission

In looking at the way Jesus ministered, we find our model for ministry today. Throughout the Gospels, we read story after story of how Jesus intersected with people — and their lives were changed forever. But Jesus was deliberate and intentional in His interaction with people. His actions may have seemed random to those observing, but when questioned, Jesus revealed His source of direction and His method of following.

In John 5, Jesus was in Jerusalem near the Bethesda pool,

where sick people awaited the stirring of the water. Whenever the water was stirred, whoever found his or her way into the pool first would be healed. On this Sabbath day, Jesus "happened" upon a man who had been an invalid for 38 years and was unable to make it into the pool first. Jesus asked the man if he wanted to get well.

> The sick man answered Him, "Sir, I have no man to put me into the pool when the water is stirred up, but while I am coming, another steps down before me. "Jesus said to him, "Get up, pick up your pallet and walk. "Immediately the man became well, and picked up his pallet and began to walk. Now it was the Sabbath on that day. — John 5:7-9

But there was an outcry from the religious sector. Jesus was healing people on the Sabbath! Almost immediately, a direct inquisition resulted, including a confrontation with Jesus. Not only was Jesus healing the man on the Sabbath, but He was telling him that there was nothing wrong with picking up his mat on the Sabbath, a taboo in the Jewish culture.

> But He answered them, "My Father is working until now, and I Myself am working." For this reason therefore the Jews were seeking all the more to kill Him, because He not only was breaking the

Sabbath, but also was calling God His own Father, making Himself equal with God. Therefore Jesus answered and was saying to them, 'Truly, truly, I say to you, the Son can do nothing of Himself, unless it is something He sees the Father doing; for whatever the Father does, these things the Son also does in like manner. For the Father loves the Son, and shows Him all things that He Himself is doing; and greater works than these will He show Him, so that you will marvel. — John 5:17-20

The truth in His words is what gives us direction on how we need to approach ministry. When the fullness that comes through the consummation of the Kingdom broke into this man's life, he was healed. And then Jesus explained how ministry works:

1. My Father is always at work.
2. On my own initiative, I can do nothing.
3. I can only do what I see the Father doing.
4. The Father loves showing Me what He is doing.

Herein lies one of the most crucial principles in understanding mission. This is how Jesus modeled ministry. Jesus walked watching. Jesus walked waiting. Jesus walked expecting to see His Father moving. (We will explore this further in chapter four.) It's often thought that when miracles in the ministry of Jesus occur, people say, "Of course, it was Jesus," as if He, in His deity and His power, conjured up these in-breakings. Yet, Paul explained that Jesus set aside His divine prerogative and lived a life dependent upon the Holy Spirit: "Have this attitude in yourselves which was also in Christ Jesus, who, although He existed in the form of God, did not regard equality with God a thing to be grasped, but emptied Himself, taking the form of a bond-servant, and being made in the likeness of men" (Philippians 2:5-7).

> *You know of Jesus of Nazareth, how God anointed Him with the Holy Spirit and with power, and how He went about doing good and healing all who were oppressed by the devil, for God was with Him.* — Acts 10:38

In John 5, we see how Jesus models a life and then gives this understanding to those who are questioning Him. When Jesus says, "My father is at work" and "The Son can do nothing of Himself," He didn't mean that He was immobile or inactive. He meant that He, just like you and me, couldn't do anything on His own power that would have eternal consequences. We can be extremely active. In fact, activism could be one of the biggest problems we have in the mission world. Without discovering what the Father is doing, we have no power behind our actions. Jesus modeled this concept and taught it. He said, "We can only do what we see the Father is doing." When we do that, our actions have divine authority with them.

After attending one of my first Vineyard conferences and listening to many stories by the speakers about how they experienced the inbreaking of God into everyday life, I was flying back to the East Coast and thought, "I've read this in a book and heard people talking about this, so I might as well give it a crack."

As I put my luggage up and began buckling up, I realized the woman on the plane next to me was clearly communicating that she wasn't interested in talking. As I attempted to engage her in a conversation, she strongly resisted. I remember praying a little prayer and asking the Lord to show me the secrets of her heart. Almost immediately the name "Mark" popped into my mind — and I was curious to see if this was something God was telling me. I asked her if the name "Mark" meant anything to her. She looked at me stunned and began to tear up. Within a few seconds, the tears were popping out and gushing down her face. Then she began quizzing me how I knew about Mark. I told her that the Lord told me and that He wanted her to know that He cares about her.

As it turned out, Mark was her nephew and his parents were getting a divorce. And this woman was broken-hearted over the way it was affecting Mark. Needless to say, from then on, we had some great conversation for the rest of the plane ride.

We need to understand this fact: God really likes showing us what He is doing. There is a peace in knowing what He is doing and participating with Him. We're on His mission, not our mission looking for His blessing. As a missional people, we are not commissioned to go out and do what we think God wants done, but we are to do what He is doing.

Receiving Direction in the Mission

Following Jesus' death and resurrection, the time had come for His ascension into heaven. As the disciples were huddled around Jesus, they anxiously wanted to know what the next step was. Where were they to go from here once their leader was gone? Finally, Jesus gave His followers the direction they had been awaiting: "But you will receive power when the Holy Spirit comes on you; and you will be my witnesses in Jerusalem, and in all Judea, and Samaria, and to the ends of the earth" (Acts 1:8).

John 5 and Acts 1:8 are tightly knit together in helping us understand how we find our mission. What does a person witness when the spirit of God comes on a believer and fills him or her with the Holy Spirit? That person begins to see what the Father is doing in a way that one may not have been able to see beforehand. The presence of the Holy Spirit in our lives is not an option or just a good thing. It's not to give us a spiritual jolt or to bring an energetic presence to a meeting. The Holy Spirit becomes the dominant power in us. Where we used to see with natural eyes, we begin to see with a different perspective. We can see how the Lord is moving and when the inbreakings are happening around us.

In Acts 2, the Holy Spirit was poured out on the church, and Peter, who had just denied Christ three times but was now filled with the Spirit, was empowered to deliver a stirring message that God had for those people at that moment. He recalled the prophecy in Joel 2 where God promised to pour out His Spirit.

> *It will come about after this that I will pour out My Spirit on all mankind; and your sons and daughters will prophesy, Your old men will dream dreams, your young men will see visions. Even on the male and female servants I will pour out My Spirit in those days.* — Joel 2:28-29

Peter received the Spirit of God, and then he was empowered to properly interpret what the Lord was doing. He began to witness the inbreaking of God and preached Jesus Christ, with thousands giving their hearts to God.

Whether in your neighborhood or in another nation, you are empowered to witness the actions of God through the power of the Holy Spirit. You will see the inbreaking of God in everyday lives. As we walk among the stop signs of life, attuned to the Holy Spirit, we witness the acts of God and testify to what we have seen. That is a missional people walking with a missional God.

Acts is a record of the apostles, and those who followed God, witnessing the inbreaking of God. Paul is not pursuing God. Paul is a persecutor wreaking havoc on the church. But missional God goes after Paul with a vengeance, knocking him off his high horse, literally. Missional God speaks to him in a heavenly language, and Paul becomes a missional person, taking up the mission of God. And that's the story of Acts. Now, let's look at Acts 29.

Chapter Three

STANDING ON THEIR SHOULDERS

Building on God's mission

*Mission is so much at the heart of the
church's life that rather than to think of it
as one aspect of its existence ... it is better to think
of it as defining its essence.*
— Andrew Kirk

ON DECEMBER 17, 1903, at Big Kill Devil Hill in Kitty Hawk, North Carolina, Orville and Wilbur Wright forever etched themselves into the history books as Orville piloted the first heavier-than-air flight. It would hardly be impressive today; but for their era, the 120-foot flight that lasted 12 seconds marked the beginning of a new era that would change the world. After years of desiring to fly, humankind had now taken the first steps toward this aeronautical triumph. However, while the Wright brothers created the functioning plane, not all their ideas about flight were their own.

As far back as the 1480s, Leonardo da Vinci began in-depth studies of flight. His flying machine, based on the same dynamics that cause birds to fly, was never recorded as being successfully created. However, his concept was used in the creation of the modern-day helicopter. And in the 19th century, when aviation pioneers began to study flight more aggressively, da Vinci's notebooks on flight were a key component in their studies.

During the first half of the 19th century, George Cayley, considered the father of aerodynamics, developed the first controllable glider. He continually improved facets of his invention, including wing design, steering rudders, tails, and rear elevators. During his studies, Cayley concluded that machine power would be necessary to sustain a long flight. His book, *On Ariel Navigation,* discussed designs for a machine-powered aircraft that would give humans the best opportunity in flight.

In the latter half of the 19th century, both Otto Lilienthal and Samuel Langley made great strides in the world of aerodynamics through intense studies. Lilienthal, who died testing one of his inventions, designed a glider that could carry a person for long distances and published a book on aerodynamics that helped the Wright brothers develop their biplane design. Langley built a plane called the aerodrome and worked hard (yet, unsuccessfully) to develop a power source for gliders.

Also in the late 1890s, Octave Chanute designed the Herring-Chanute biplane from which the Wright brothers designed their successful biplane. Chanute's book entitled, *Progress in Flying Machines,* helped the Wright brothers in their flight experiments.

As the Wright brothers began to progress in the quest to develop a successful plane, they relied heavily upon the works of Cayley, Langley, and Lilienthal, and corresponded with Chanute regarding some of their innovations with the plane. Though the Wright brothers finished the job of making flight for mankind possible, they stood on the shoulders of many great innovators before them.[1]

Acts 29

Don't look too hard — you won't find a 29th chapter in Acts, nor was there one ever written for the Bible. However, that next chapter is still being written as we stand on the shoulders of those faithful men and women who have carried the torch of faith down through the ages. Beginning with Abram, Israel, and the first century church, missional God has continued throughout history His work of redemption, reaching into the sea of humanity and picking men and women to impact the world in which they live. God continues to interrupt people's lives with a mission from heaven.

As we study heroes of the faith and how they have impacted the world, we must remember one thing: God is still the star of the show. People who have lived lives of obedience and suffered for the sake of the Gospel throughout the annals of time all share a common denominator. Missional God is the one who interrupted their lives and gave them a new direction. Players have come and gone, but God is the one who has stayed the course throughout history.

Despite our penchant for viewing ourselves as innovators in the 21st century, we must realize that we aren't as in vogue as we think. Instead of blazing trails with our faith, we have taken the torch that has been passed down from generation to generation. We are a family of torch bearers. I've told those who are thinking about church planting that what they've actually become a part of is a fraternity of torch bearers for their generation. That's the essence of Acts 29.

The Wright brothers were the first to take off, but they learned some things from the mistakes of others in launching. Many times when great things are accomplished, we look at those who achieved the breakthrough, praising them without remembering those who helped lay the ground work. Choosing to continue the work of those who have gone before us causes humility in us as we realize what we have done is follow in the steps of greatness. If we do reap a harvest, we understand that we are harvesting the seeds of both present and past generations.

First Corinthians 4:7 states, "What do you have that you did not receive?" If a person does a great thing with his or her life, it's because he or she has received an empowerment to do that in the context of his or her life. And when we talk about great men and women of God, what made them great was their willingness to be used and do what God called them to do, following in the footsteps of those who had walked before them.

An Unlikely Direction

At the age of 16, Patrick was ripped from his family by a band of marauding Druids, who stormed through England as the Roman Empire withdrew — raping, murdering, and plundering the land. Raised in a nominal Christian family, Patrick had no idea what to expect as he was placed under the protection of one of the band of warriors. Suddenly, Patrick's daily life consisted of tending flocks in the hills of

Ireland for these plundering thieves. During those nights on the hills of Ireland, Patrick began to powerfully encounter God. Instead of being a distant entity, God became real to Patrick. No longer was Patrick alone. There was an intimacy in relationship, the sense that God cared about him. And one night, God spoke clearly to Patrick, telling him to escape and return home. So, Patrick did just that, finding his way back to England.

Upon returning home, he began to prepare himself for a life of ministry as he reacquainted himself with his family. Though it felt good to be home, Patrick sensed there was a calling on his life. And not long afterward, Patrick had another experience where the Lord used an Irishman named Victorious to speak to him in a dream. Victoricus asked him to come back and live among his people. After joining a monastery in Gaul on the island of Lérins, Patrick returned to Ireland.

By some accounts, he was considered one of the first missionaries to leave the Roman Empire for the advancement of God's Kingdom. He became a spiritual father to Ireland. He came to a pagan Ireland and, upon his death, had planted hundreds of faith communities, leading thousands to faith in Jesus Christ.[2]

During that particular time, St. Patrick was one of the bright lights the Lord used. Throughout the reign of the Roman Empire, we read about those who were writers of Christian doctrine and theology, wrestling with the issues of God and faith. And then there were others dying for their faith. Perpetua, in the beginning of the third century, with her friend Felicitus, was martyred for her faith. She said, "When a person is given a last name, that is who they are. That's simply who they are."[3] She laid down her life and carried a torch for Jesus Christ.

Now, it would be easy for someone to say that Patrick had a most unfortunate turn of circumstances, violently removed from his family and forced to spend six years in exile from them. His family surely lived tormented, wondering whether young Patrick was dead or alive. But now that history has run its course, Patrick would look back and say that God was positioning him for what was next. God can peek around the corner and we can't. God intended for this young man to bear the torch for Jesus Christ in a difficult moment in Europe. Things that Patrick learned about missional God are things that help us as we embark on a mission for God.

During his time of captivity, Patrick learned the native tongue and then the Gaelic language. When he came back with his team many years later, Patrick was able to address the people in their native tongue — something that showed he went out of his way to learn their ways, to understand their ways, and be a part of who they were. Patrick learned the importance of contextualization within another person's culture.

But it was God who was on the mission. He used Patrick to reverse their situation, a providential reversal. If we continued through history, we could study the time of the crusades. Francis of Assisi had come to a place of knowing the Lord, yet his desire to spread the Gospel outside of his native home-land of Italy was frustrated many times. It was Francis who, upon reaching the Middle East, asked for permission to cross the front lines of battle. At an agreed upon time, he was allowed to minister to the Sultan of Egypt during a time when Christians were battling and killing Muslims. He ministered during a time when the love of God was not being administered by the church. Francis believed that it was the church's duty to show the love of Christ in a practical way. During that time, Francis carried the torch of the love of God.

During the time of barbarians, there were many people who were heroes as well. Who were the "missionaries" at that time? When the Vikings made a sweep through England and into Europe, they annihilated people. Yet, they took many monks to be teachers and women to be wives — and those people stayed true to their faith, ministering to those who held them captive. They were missionaries in their own essence.

In his book *The Last of the Giants,* George Otis tells the incredible story of Raymond Lull, a Spanish missionary from the 14th century who is generally regarded as the first missionary to Muslims. Lull wrote in his book *The Tree of Life,* that in order to break through the Islamic faith, one must do so "by love and prayers, and the pouring out of tears and blood." He was martyred in a village east of Algiers in June of 1315. Almost 600 years later, one night an entire village experienced dreams and visions as well as angelic visitations. The next morning, every person shared the story of what happened to them during the night — and they realized they needed Jesus. Over the following weeks, almost the entire village of more than 400 people gave their hearts to Jesus. Though it was centuries later, the harvest of the seeds Lull sowed were finally reaped.[4]

Now, who was on a mission there? Lull was available and on the scene, and then missional God brought some ends together. In one sense, it was both — but the dramatic conversion of that village occurred because God was on the relentless pursuit of the hearts of those village people. Lull laid the groundwork, giving his entire life. And God closed the deal. We have to understand that the Gospel message has been carried through the ages on the shoulders of those saints who have gone before us.

If we look into the period of time called the "Reformation" when the Word of God was being given back to the church, we have one of those strong movements in which God performed a miraculous thing with the Moravians in the 18th century. A small band of disenfranchised people gathered together to pray in Herrnhut, Saxony, in Germany on Count Zinzendorf's estate. They began to pray for their people and for God's Spirit to be poured out among them — and the people began a continual prayer meeting that continued 24 hours a day for over 100 years![5] That's a work of God. God initiated it, but the people carried it out.

No matter who he or she is in whatever empire or whatever period of history — the Wesleys, the Whitefields, the van

Zinzendorfs—the whole point is that all of these people come and go from these scenes, but we see the church pushed forward into modern mission. God is the constant throughout time.

Four Men, Three Eras, One Mission

In the first era of modern missions (1782-1865), becoming a missionary was synonymous with becoming a martyr. Missionaries who went to Africa after 1790 left their homelands with great passion; yet few missionaries survived longer than a few years. In fact, the missionaries packed their belongings in coffins because they knew they wouldn't be going home.

At my son-in-law's college graduation a few years ago, I visited a missionary museum in Tulsa, Oklahoma. I was struck by the emotion and the sanctity of it as I walked through the halls, a visual tribute to those who paid a great price through the ages. As I turned a corner, I remember coming upon a big display on Africa. Leaning up against the wall was a long, rectangular, wooden box fashioned after one of the crates used to ship goods from England to Africa that doubled as a coffin for the missionaries. These people knew they had a short season for their lives, but they walked into it because they were arrested by the Spirit. They were willing to spend their brief hour on the earth for the people of Africa. God was on a mission, and He used those people to fulfill it.

In the late 1700s, a young man named William Carey sat in his cobbler shop in England, thinking about taking the Gospel around the world. When he challenged the leaders of the church at that time, they told him God would win the heathens without his help. Undaunted, he considered how he could carry the Gospel to the world in his generation. In 1793, Carey, along with some of his friends, formed the Baptist Home Mission Society, and Carey left as a missionary for India.

Just as the torch has been passed from generation to generation within the context of our faith, likewise it has been passed in missions. Hudson Taylor, who was heavily influenced by the messages and writings of Carey, began to feel a burden for, and raise awareness of, the people in China who had never heard the Gospel. **In this second era of modern missions** (1865-1934), Taylor began to confront the church leaders about their apparent lack of interest in taking the Gospel to inland China. However, the response he received was a harsh warning, as these leaders told Taylor that the blood of these young missionaries would be on his hands. Taylor, being somewhat discouraged, was comforted by God as the Lord told him, "You are not calling people to China. I am."

Taylor eventually founded the China Inland Mission, which exposed young men and women to the need for missionaries in the interior of China. And the response was overwhelming. As he made an appeal to church leaders across the globe to send missionaries to China, Taylor sought 1,000 men and women to share the Gospel in a nation hungry for the truth. Working with a number of different organizations, Taylor saw the 1,000 he dreamed of make their way to China. In fact, it was over 1,150 when it was all said and done![6] Taylor was one man used by God to further His mission to draw the hearts of men and women unto Himself.

In the latest era of modern missions (1934-present), more people have come to Christ than in all the previous centuries of Christianity. The torch bearers who have picked up the torch from each previous generation have done so with passion and fervor. The 20th century missions were led by a man who, among others, accepted the invitation to advance the Kingdom of God: Cameron Townsend.

Townsend, who quit college to answer the call of God, headed off to Guatemala to spread the Gospel before he realized how many of the people he was ministering to didn't even speak Spanish. Early in his days on the mission field in Guatemala, a Cakchiquel Indian wanted to know why, if Townsend's God was so smart, He couldn't speak their language. Returning to the United States, Townsend founded Wycliffe Bible Translators in 1942, which today employs 5,000 people who are administering the Gospel all over the world.[7]

Donald McGavran, another major contributor in this era, helped usher in a paradigm shift from thinking about missions in the context of geography to the context of people groups. The church must adapt to the people and their context. By observing the different caste systems in India, McGavran brought to the world's awareness this whole concept of separation of people. He recognized that people were not separated geographically as much as they were separated culturally and linguistically.

Rooted deep within McGavran's missiology was also his commitment to church planting. He believed the local church was essential to take missions from simply an introduction to the Gospel to a fervent application of it. Upon baptizing the first converted Hindu into the Christian faith, McGavran watched his India mission begin to grow to hundreds of believers becoming active in local churches established there.[8]

Perpetua, Constantine, Francis, Lull, Taylor, Carey, Townsend, McGavran — these people through the centuries have walked with God, and we walk on their shoulders.

Beginning with Jesus and His small band of believers in Israel, we see a passing of the torch through a 2,000-year period — the persecution of the Roman Empire, the Dark Ages, the Crusades (one of the biggest black eyes in Christian history) and to modern times. There has always been a testimony to Jesus Christ in the world. There has always been a God on a mission.

We see that He is on a mission. He is successful on His mission. He has called out a people, and there is a fraternity of torch bearers through the centuries. Now, it's a challenge to us. How does that apply to the guy today in the average church? Does that mean I have to be martyred or go off to another place?

In his book, *Mission on the Way,* Chuck van Engen writes, "Mission is the people of God intentionally crossing barriers from church to non-church, faith to non-faith, to proclaim by word and deed the coming of the Kingdom of God in Jesus Christ; this task is achieved by means of the church's participation in God's mission of reconciling people to God, to themselves, to each other, and to the world, and gathering them into the church through repentance and faith in Jesus Christ by the work of the Holy Spirit with a view to the transformation of the world as a sign of the coming of the Kingdom in Jesus Christ."[9]

In missions, the issue is not geography or profession, but realizing that because we confess Jesus as our Savior, then God's mission becomes our mission. Does that mean geographical barriers? Does it mean crossing the street? Crossing the doorway to the next house? Missions is not about crossing any of these barriers as much as it is about guiding unbelieving people from non-faith to faith.

I don't know a better way to conclude this chapter than to simply and humbly thank God for those who have paid the price for the Gospel to advance to the place that it is in today's world. Many have gone before us. Now, it's our turn. He is on a mission. We are His people. We are invited to be a part of the historical fraternity. And now we must discover what God is doing and where He is doing it in our day.

Notes

1. Scott, Phil. *The Shoulders of Giants*. Reading, Massachusetts: Addison-Wesley Publishing, 1995.

2. Cahill, Thomas. *How the Irish Saved Civilisation: The Untold Story of the Fall of Rome to the Rise of Medieval Europe*. New York: Double Day, 1995.

3. Gonzalez, Justo. *The Story of Christianity: Volume One: The Early Church to the Reformation.* San Francisco: Harper, 1984.

4. Otis, George. *The Last of the Giants.* Grand Rapids, Michigan: Chosen Books, 1991.

5. Johnson, Nita. "The First Great Global Awakening of the 1700s." Teaching on Revival. http://www.world-forjesus.org/home/teaching_articles.cfm?ID=51 Retrieved September 2003

6. Taylor, Dr. Howard. *J. Hudson Taylor: God's Man in China.* Chicago: Moody Press, 1965.

7. Winter, Ralph D. *Perspectives on the World Christian Movement: A Reader.* Waynesboro, Georgia: Gabriel Resources, 1999.

8. Ibid.

9. Van Engen, Charles. *Mission on the Way: Issues in Mission Theology.* Grand Rapids, Michigan: Baker Book House, 1997.

Chapter Four

DISCOVERING GOD AT WORK

Seeing what the
Father is doing

The greatest obstacle is discovery
is not ignorance — it is the illusion of knowledge.
— Daniel J. Boorstin

ONCE WHILE I WAS speaking at a missions seminar in Boise, Idaho, a woman bubbling with joy came bounding up to me between sessions. She could hardly wait to tell the story of her friend Jane that explicitly demonstrated what was just taught during the previous session.

Standing in line at the supermarket, Jane was waiting for her turn until it was time to check out. She had no idea that she was about to enter a life-altering situation for an unsuspecting woman. While Jane stood patiently in line, the young woman in front of her emptied her basket and waited for the total from the cashier, which came to a total of $45.10. Immediately, the young woman began rifling through her purse and quickly became flustered: she couldn't find her debit card — and her wallet had no cash.

Jane observed the situation and offered assistance. She told the clerk, "Put those groceries on my check!"

The young woman turned to Jane and said, "Why are you doing that? People don't do things like that!"

"Well, I go to a really cool church and we do that. We try to change the world and make a difference by doing simple acts of kindness. And I want to do this for you," Jane said.

Stunned by this kindness, the young woman turned around and loudly began announcing to the rest of people in the checkout area what Jane had done, much to Jane's embarrassment. Once Jane finished buying her groceries, the young woman walked her out to her car. She asked Jane where she went to church because she wanted to attend. The young woman said she didn't know anyone who would have done such a thing — and she wanted to visit a church made up of people who would.

Now, here's my question: Was Jane out doing grocery shopping evangelism? Or was Jane out among the stop signs of life and recognized God at work? Jane saw missional God in this unlikely opportunity standing in line at the grocery store. In fact, Jane recognized that mission isn't something you go and do as much as it is being opportunistic in sharing the Gospel. Jane was being missional without even trying.

The Art of Discovery

As we study the scripture, a defining truth is exposed concerning Jesus' ministry on earth: He followed God with explicit obedience. Jesus had no agenda of His own. He was not seeking to gain political power or overwhelm the masses with incredible popularity. A case could even be made that Jesus was the most unassuming man to walk the planet. The number one agenda in Jesus' life was discovering what Father God was already doing and join Him.

In the book of John, we find Jesus ministering in a way

that wasn't quite pleasing to the Jewish leaders of the day. Jesus had just healed a lame man at the pool of Bethesda on the Sabbath, and they were all over His case. Yet, in this story, we find Jesus explaining the essence of missions, which bears repeating:

> For this reason the Jews were persecuting Jesus, because He was doing these things on the Sabbath. But He answered them, "My Father is working until now, and I Myself am working." For this reason therefore the Jews were seeking all the more to kill Him, because He not only was breaking the Sabbath, but also was calling God His own Father, making Himself equal with God. Therefore Jesus answered and was saying to them, "Truly, truly, I say to you, the Son can do nothing of Himself, unless it is something He sees the Father doing, for whatever the Father does, these things the Son also does in like manner. For the Father loves the Son, and shows Him all things that He Himself is doing; and the Father will show Him greater works than these, so that you will marvel. — John 5:16-20

In becoming missional people, we must understand the elements that comprise God's mission and enable us to participate with Him. Jesus, the Son of God, laid aside His divine prerogative when He came to earth and operated dependent upon the power of the Holy Spirit. And it was that empowerment that allowed Him to understand, see, and hear exactly what the Father was doing. I briefly mentioned these four principles in chapter two, but they are paramount to our understanding of God's mission. So, let's take a closer look.

My Father Is Always at Work

Every time we read the verses above, we understand that God the Father is always at work. This is not the first time we find this in Scripture. 2 Chronicles 16:9 says, "For the eyes of the Lord move to and fro throughout the earth that He may strongly support those whose heart is completely His." God is always at work. In fact, there is not a time when the Lord isn't at work. This is why thinking about missions as a way of discovering what the Lord is doing becomes a crucial aspect of participating in God's mission. Whether in the street, the nations, or the world, we must realize that it is not up to us to create something but to discover what God is already doing. As mentioned earlier, Jane at the supermarket wasn't trying to create a situation; rather, she realized that the Lord was opening the door for her. She needed to be sensitive and offered a kind gesture, which allowed her to enter into the life of someone. I guarantee that God was working in that woman's life before she encountered Jane in the grocery store.

Another young woman I know named Ellen was sitting in

an airplane on the tarmac when the captain announced takeoff would be delayed because of fast-moving thunderstorms. Instead of huffing over an unknown length in delay, Ellen struck up a conversation with a young woman next to her named Elizabeth. The two women discovered they had much in common, except for the issue of faith. Ellen was a devout Christian, and Elizabeth was still searching for answers in her faith.

As Elizabeth began to share about her Catholic upbringing, she raised questions about why she couldn't talk to God directly and confess her sins to Him. She wanted to know why she couldn't have a personal relationship with God.

Ellen seized the opportunity and began sharing what it meant to have a personal relationship with the Lord. For over an hour, Ellen shared her faith. Four hours later, the plane finally took off. Though worn out from sitting in the plane for six hours, Ellen refused to complain, feeling as if God had somehow orchestrated everything, including the seating arrangement and the "sudden" thunderstorms.

And Ellen's hunches were correct. Ellen and Elizabeth exchanged contact information, including an e-mail site where Elizabeth could receive daily devotionals. A month later, Ellen received an e-mail from one of Elizabeth's friends who had been praying for opportunities to share her faith with Elizabeth for quite some time — and had also subscribed to the devotional upon Elizabeth's suggestion. Elizabeth's conversation with Ellen opened up new doors for her friend to talk with her about her Christian faith.

We know the Lord was already working in the life of Elizabeth by the fact that, when Ellen received an e-mail, we discover there was another Christian involved in Elizabeth's life, interceding for her. Was Ellen involved in airplane evangelism? Ellen saw an invitation to speak life into a thirsty soul and charged ahead. In that moment, Ellen discovered what God was doing and chose to be a willing participant.

The whole issue in missions is not us trying to do something for God but, rather, discovering what He is doing.

On My Own Initiative, I Can Do Nothing

The Son can do nothing of Himself. Jesus explains that He can't do anything that has an eternal, positive effect in the life of people on His own strength. That gives us the picture of Him being dependent upon God's guidance and direction as opposed to an independent do-gooder on a crusade to save the world.

Jesus laid aside His divine prerogative in order to be dependent upon His Father. Many people will look at the things that Jesus has done and say, "Well, of course, He can do that because He was the son of God." That comment infers that Jesus operated totally out of His divinity while walking on the earth. However, that is far from what actually happened. God anointed Jesus with the Holy Spirit and with power to do the Father's will — and Jesus went about doing good works and healing all those who were oppressed.

In healing the man by the pool at Bethesda, Jesus didn't

operate on His own accord. Jesus explained that He could only do what He saw God doing. He said "I can't do this. I can only do what I see the Father doing."

In the middle of Acts, we find Peter grasping this principle with diligence. With the Holy Spirit fully unleashed in the earth, Peter is operating on a different level than he has in the past. Peter waltzes into the home of Cornelius, a Roman officer — something that was taboo according to Jewish law.

> *And he said to them, 'You yourselves know how unlawful it is for a man who is a Jew to associate with a foreigner or to visit him; and yet God has shown me that I should not call any man unholy or unclean.'* — Acts 10:28

This was not biblical law that Peter was breaking, but the laws of man — laws that were written by man and for man. Yet in his sensitivity to the Holy Spirit, Peter learns that when he is listening to God, he can begin to do and act as God would have him to do and act.

It often seems like everybody wants a miracle, but nobody wants to be in a place where they need one. Yet, it is in our desperate need of a miracle that God makes His presence known, oftentimes using people to accomplish His will.

While I was a missionary in Chile, I had come to a place where I had run out of ways to provide for my family. We received money from outside the country through missionary support, which resulted in a monthly stipend. But through various circumstances, we were out of resources. One morning as our children left for school, my wife and I knew we needed a miracle to feed them upon their return. Not only was our cupboard cleaned out, but so was our bank account.

I went to the church like always and, upon my arrival, received a notice that a package had arrived for me at customs. I went to the customs office and picked up a book that someone had sent me from the United States. When I got back to my office, I began thumbing through the book and found a $50 bill the sender had placed in the book for me. When I looked at the postage date on the package, I realized my friend had sent this package almost three months earlier — and it arrived on the day I literally had run out of money.

I knew I had no ability or power to generate a miracle like that in order to fulfill my responsibility as a father and husband to provide for my family. But God knew. He pressed upon the heart of an obedient man to send us money — and it came in our moment of dire need. While those situations magnify the truth of our dependency upon the Lord, they also magnify the importance for us to be obedient when God asks us to do something that is far from our own accord. What may have seemed like a simple gesture of kindness to the man who sent us money was actually God intervening in our family's life, showing how much He cared for our needs. Instead of manufacturing opportunities to show God's love, we begin to learn how to discover what

God is doing as well as what He wants us to do.

Jesus stressed this point: "I can't do anything on my own accord." That has been a reality in my own life as well, as I have failed miserably to produce things on my own that could make a difference, and succeeded exceedingly when I obeyed God's leading.

I Can Only Do What I See the Father Doing

This aspect of Jesus' teaching is one of the foundational teaching blocks that John Wimber, the founder of the Vineyard movement, drilled home on so many occasions: we can only do what we see the Father doing. This truth became a real staple for me, not only in my theology during my early years of ministry, but also in my ministry practice.

A few years ago on a brief mission trip to Monterrey, Mexico, I was sharing the pulpit with a friend of mine at a week-long conference. I was praying about what to say when, suddenly, the Lord began to give me personal words about the people of Monterrey. During my second night of preaching, I felt prompted to look at my notes and share some of the personal words God had given me for the people. I shared that there was a family in attendance that was quite wealthy but was in the process of losing everything — and the Lord wanted them to know He would walk with them through this dark valley. Upon sharing that word, I knew I was now on the spot because I explicitly said, "The Lord said that to me."

At the end of the service after praying for hundreds of people, a middle-aged woman came up to me and shared with me the details of her family's trouble. As you might suspect, it was exactly as God showed me. Her family had been an extremely wealthy industrial family — and they were on the verge of losing everything. She asked me to speak to the entire family. I then went to her family and shared with them. The only thing I was led to give them was hope that God knew about them and that He wanted to keep them in a place of hope. I didn't know the family or the situation, but I knew that's what the Father was doing, which resulted in my participation in God's mission for the hearts of this particular family.

In seeking to grasp this concept, we begin to understand more about Jesus and the way He operated on earth. Jesus could see what the Father was doing because the Holy Spirit was revealing knowledge to Him. Jesus lived in a power outside of His humanity, so He could see, perceive, and understand what the Father was doing. While this may sound too lofty of a concept to grasp, the power who availed Himself to Jesus 2,000 years ago is available to us today. What joy to know that we, too, can operate under the same guidance that led Jesus!

What's also important to understand is that the Holy Spirit doesn't play favorites, revealing plans to some and not others. You don't have to be a pastor or a missionary or an evangelist to find out what the Father is doing. In grasping this fundamental lesson to become missional people, there are four things we need.

1. **Desire.** Is there a desire in your heart to see God work through your life? The Lord is looking for able-bodied Christians who are willing to serve in order to advance His Kingdom. Even if you do not desire to participate in what God is doing, He remains ready to help you. "For it is God who is at work in you both to will and to work for His good pleasure" (Philippians 2:13). Our desire determines, to some degree, how much we will be involved in God's mission.

2. **Expectancy.** Do you believe God is really at work around you? Are you ever expectant that God is ready to work through you and around you? If we do not expect God to work, it may sometimes take a dramatic wake-up call for us to see what He is doing. However, when we live in a constant state of expectancy, excited about His next move around us, we will be able to more easily hear and see what He is doing.

3. **Staying filled.** While you may have experienced an encounter with the Holy Spirit where you yielded your life to the work of the Lord, are you living daily in the power of the Holy Spirit? Paul encouraged the church in Ephesus to "be filled with the Spirit" (Ephesians 5:18). Are you being filled anew each day with the Holy Spirit's power? I don't know how many times throughout my years in ministry that I've heard people say, "I got the baptism many years ago." It's great that they have had an experience, but are they walking in that power each day? Before your feet hit the floor each morning, you have to have an attitude that says, "I want to live a life committed to You, Lord. I want to see what You

are doing. I know You are involved in my life. Give me the eyes to see what You are doing today."

4. **A secret life.** Do you make a point to spend time alone with God each day? Throughout the book of Luke, we see over and over Jesus' dependency upon the Father. Oftentimes, Jesus arose early in the morning and disappeared into the wilderness to spend time with God. "When day came, Jesus left and went to a secluded place; and the crowds were searching for Him, and came to Him and tried to keep Him from going away from them" (Luke 4:42). However, Jesus knew that in order to give the people what they needed, He must first spend time with God.

We see how Jesus emphasizes this fact even as His popularity spread: "But the news about Him was spreading even farther, and large crowds were gathering to hear Him and to be healed of their sicknesses. But Jesus Himself would often slip away to the wilderness and pray" (Luke 5:15-16). In our culture today, whenever someone performs great miracles, we rent a stadium, sign a book deal, and make tapes and CDs. But as Jesus' fame became more intense, He slipped into the wilderness to pray. He believed that overflow of intimacy with His Father was the way to advance the Kingdom. By spending time alone with God, we receive the life we need in order to give it away.

A secret life ties into intimacy. Ministry and mission must come from overflow of intimacy in our time with God. If we overwork ourselves, we will begin operating out of duty, which is not what God wants. He wants us to advance His Kingdom out of love for Him and our joy that we find in relationship with Him.

In Luke 6, we find Jesus taking seriously the selection of 12 apostles from His disciples. "It was at this time that He went off to the mountain to pray, and He spent the whole night in prayer to God. And when day came, He called His disciples to Him and chose twelve of them, whom He also named as apostles" (Luke 6:12-13). He spent the entire night in prayer to make that weighty decision — these would be the men He chose to carry out His teachings from generation to generation. He didn't just say, "I have a personality rapport with these guys, so I will pick them."

He spent the entire night in prayer, asking God who God wanted. Jesus' secret life with the heavenly Father resulted in wisdom to advance God's Kingdom.

However, there is no formula to knowing what the Father is doing. It is based on relationship. Knowing what the Father is doing is not rocket science, nor is it a procedure. As we seek to know God more, we will know naturally more about what He is doing and be able to participate in His plan to redeem the lives of those around us.

The Father Loves Showing Me What He Is Doing

God shows us what He is doing as we delve into a deeper relationship with Him. What we discover is that we are not taking God somewhere — He is taking us to where He is already working. In the context of being missional people, this concept remains the same whether you are crossing the street or crossing continents where you must penetrate geographical, cultural, and linguistic barriers. God is already there.

Don Richardson, a missionary to Sawi people of Irian Jaya in the 1960s and 70s, found God already at work in an area that seemed forsaken. The Sawi culture was one of the most dangerous in the world, melding headhunting and cannibalism into a way of life. Sharing the Gospel with these people was a formidable task, especially considering their savage way of living. Don grew frustrated in his efforts to convey the Gospel message to them: "In their eyes Judas, not Jesus, was the hero of the Gospel. Jesus was just the dupe to be laughed at." But God was already preparing the hearts of the Sawi people — and one day He showed Don what He was doing.

Through Don's efforts to bring unity among three tribal villages, he had also brought together three savage tribes which took aim at rival tribe members and killed one another. Distraught, Don decided the best decision was for him and his wife to leave the jungle and let the tribal villages return to living in isolation. The Sawi people were disappointed to hear of the Richardsons' impending exit from their villages. They called a tribal session that would bring peace and keep the Richardsons from leaving.

As the diplomatic process began among the Sawi people, Don began to see the way the Father was already at work. In order to make peace, some of the families traded children with rival tribes, knowing that if their child was alive, peace reigned in the region. Don realized that if these villagers could hand over their own children to a man from a rival tribe, they could actually trust the man from the rival tribe. Through that analogy, Don was able to explain the Gospel truth. In fact, the truth had been there all along — God just used Don to open the eyes of the Sawi people to see it and introduce them to Jesus![1]

We sometimes operate with the mistaken notion that mission is about us taking God to those poor people who don't have God. However, God is actively at work among Muslims, Buddhists, secular humanists, atheists, and Hindus. As we fully grasp the prototype model of ministry Jesus used, we find that Jesus was just participating in what God was already doing. We may cross many different barriers or simply the street in front of our house; but when we get there, we will find that the Father is alive and well there, working in the hearts of those people to draw them unto Himself.

The Father loves to show us what He is doing. He is not hiding His plans from us. Whether church planting in Muslim countries in the Middle East, or Buddhist areas in Asia, or among the Smiths and the Joneses next door, we find God at work. Mission is simply extending God's heart to all people — people whom He is already stirring.

As we think about discovering what the Father is doing, we want to be careful to avoid sitting on our hands as we wait for the next big revival to hit the planet. This is what I like to refer to as the "Big Bang" theory of evangelism. Whether it's meant to be communicated by our itinerant evangelists or not, we seem to constantly hear, "Revival is around the corner." I have no problems with that, but my challenge is that we do not sit around waiting for it to happen. We have to remember that God is always working, whether out in the open on center stage, or veiled behind the curtains and a shadowy backdrop.

God can both sovereignly pour out His Spirit and work overtly, and He can also work covertly behind the scenes. But we cannot wait for a massive outpouring to advance His Kingdom. We must act now. We must expect God to be working in our lives on a regular basis until Jesus returns. Whether you are a teacher, a mechanic, a carpenter, a doctor, a lawyer, a housewife, or a salesman, you have to have an expectancy that God is at work around you, not just in a baseball stadium with a world-famous preacher at a meeting. Look and see what God is doing around you and accept His invitation to get involved.

In reflecting upon the whole issue that God the Father is always at work and we need to discover what is happening, we are introduced to our next principle in life with missional God: the difference between witnessing and being a witness.

Notes

1. Tucker, Ruth. *From Jerusalem to Irian Jaya*. Grand Rapids, Michigan: Zondervan, 1983.

Chapter Five

WITNESSING VERSUS BEING A WITNESS

How to witness the acts of God to others

*Time is precious, but truth
is more precious than time.*
— Benjamin Disraeli

UNLESS THE GIFT OF EVANGELISM ranks high on your list of spiritual gifts, you probably start to get a dry mouth and shudder when you hear the word "witness." Though you know you are supposed to witness to others about the love of God, it rarely conjures up happy thoughts. The fear of rejection may first come to mind, as well as the inability to know what to say to the person in front of you. But I think there is a distinct difference between witnessing and being a witness.

For example, we have heard many stories about the dangerous voyages people endured when they crossed the Atlantic Ocean to reach America. And while the stories we have heard or even seen depicted seem grotesque, hearing it from someone who was on those ships gives us a new appreciation for what the ancestors of the United States endured.

Consider crossing the Atlantic Ocean from the eyes of a man on one of those ships — Gottleb Mittelberger, an organ master and school teacher who made his way to America in 1750:

> *During the voyage there is on board these ships terrible misery, stench, fumes, horror, vomiting, many kinds of seasickness, fever,*

dysentery, headache, heat, constipation, boils, scurvy, cancer, mouth rot, and the like, all of which come from old and sharply-salted food and meat, also from very bad and foul water, so that many die miserably.

Add to this want of provisions, hunger, thirst, frost, heat, dampness, anxiety, want, afflictions and lamentations, together with other trouble, as e.g., the lice abound so frightfully, especially on sick people, that they can be scraped off the body. The misery reaches a climax when a gale rages for two or three nights and days, so that every one believes that the ship will go to the bottom with all human beings on board. In such a visitation the people cry and pray most piteously.

When the ships have landed at Philadelphia after their long voyage, no one is permitted to leave them except those who pay for their passage or can give good security; the others, who cannot pay, must remain on board the ships till they are purchased and are released from the ships by their purchasers. The sick always fare the worst, for the healthy are naturally preferred and purchased first; and so the sick and wretched must often remain on board in front of the city for two or three weeks, and

*frequently die, whereas many a one, if he could
pay his debt and were permitted to leave the
ship immediately, might recover and remain
alive."*

Such a story carries more weight when it comes from
someone who spent nearly five months crossing the Atlantic
Ocean on one of those ships. Likewise, as we witness the
power of God on a regular basis, our story not only becomes
more powerful, but it openly demonstrates God's love in an
undeniable way.

God's Ambassadors

As we see more clearly the mission that God is on, we begin
to understand that God has always had representative people
throughout the ages. Understanding what the Father is
doing is the model Jesus' ministry gives us. And it is the only
effective model that God's ambassadors have used.

In Acts 1:8, Jesus explained the next step to the disciples:
"But you will receive power when the Holy Spirit has come
upon you; and you shall be My witnesses both in Jerusalem,
and in all Judea and Samaria, and even to the remotest part
of the earth."

There are two things Jesus is doing here. First, He is
ministering in the context of His life and the lives of the people living there at that time. These disciples, listening to
Jesus, live in this area of the world and will spread the Gospel

to their people first before going beyond this region. Second, He is ministering with an eternal perspective in mind. These witnesses are going to be telling the world about the power of God for generations to come. They are going to be doing the Lord's bidding when Jesus ascends into heaven. Whether they realized it or not, these disciples were to be sent out as ambassadors of God.

In John 20:21, Jesus passed the torch: "Peace be with you; as the Father has sent me, I also send you." Jesus saw the Father sending these disciples out to the nations to declare His salvation and truth, so Jesus sent them.

When the disciples were told to wait in the upper room until they were endued with power from on high by the Lord, Jesus knew what they needed: they needed the power of the Holy Spirit in order to experience the same rich relationship with God that He had experienced while on earth. He knew they would not be able to operate in the Kingdom of God without that relationship.

However, the disciples were not sure what this power was going to look like. In fact, they still held out hope that Jesus was going to exert the Kingdom of God on Israel through a political path. "So when they had come together, they were asking Him, saying, 'Lord, is it at this time You are restoring the kingdom to Israel?'" (Acts 1:6). And that's when Jesus spells it out for them — that they are going to receive the power to carry out the Kingdom of God.

This is a crucial launching pad in understanding ministry

and mission. Jesus said, "You shall receive power." The word "power" here in the Greek is *dunamis* or "a power beyond yourself." Once you receive that power, you are an ambassador of Christ, a witness.

Witnessing Versus Being a Witness: The Difference

Historically, in the church when we have talked about witnessing, we assume that we are to be sharing our faith, our apologetics — telling people about God who may not know the Lord. But let's look at it differently.

In our premise from the previous chapter, we learned that we can only do something that we see the Father doing. In my natural strength, I can't witness the acts of God on my own because I can't see them. But when I receive the power of the Holy Spirit, I then witness the acts of God, and I can interpret what is going on. I don't have a problem with witnessing about God, but I do have a problem when the church uses Acts 1:8 as if this is witnessing with steroids. I think that's missing the point. When we try to witness to someone about the power of God when we are not experiencing it ourselves, we are passing along a story we have heard rather than the power of God we have witnessed firsthand.

During my second year of Bible college, we were required to select a nearby community, gather some people and begin teaching a Bible study there. Many of the young students were eager to go into surrounding areas and put into practice some of the lessons we had learned, myself included. The community I chose was Lanesboro, Massachusetts. As I began this assignment, I started out with great faith every Saturday morning. I had acquired maps of the streets and familiarized myself with the community's layout. For many Saturdays, I went door to door to witness for Jesus. I was determined to start a Bible study. In my naiveté, I thought the good people of Lanesboro were just waiting for me to come to them and show them how to find a relationship with God. But after a few weeks, all I had accomplished was getting bitten by a dog on my leg and having numerous doors slammed in my face.

While I coerced one man to join my Bible study and learned an important lesson about faithfulness, the fact of the matter was that I was ill-equipped. I thought I had to create something and work hard to get some momentum behind it. But over time, I have come to realize that I was simply witnessing about God instead of powerfully witnessing the acts of God.

Just like the story told at the opening of this chapter, stories that are told from the people who have been there, done that, and seen the events unfold before their very eyes hold the most weight. Stories told in vague generalities immediately reveal themselves as something that wasn't experienced first-hand — and the power of the story fades ever so slightly.

As we begin reading Acts 1, we see the drama unfolding in Peter's life. Just a short while ago, Peter had denied even knowing Jesus. Peter had neither the spiritual understanding to know what was happening, nor the stamina to make it through the trials to know that He wasn't faithful. He didn't even have the insight at that moment to know what was happening. He had glimpses, but he didn't understand the fullness. Peter still did not have the indwelling of the Holy Spirit in his life as a sense of empowerment.

So, here is Peter who did not understand what was happening at the betrayal and the arrest and the trials. But then in the upper room, Peter, disillusioned and heart-broken, is waiting on the Lord with the other disciples. During their wait, they were baptized by the Holy Spirit into the body of Christ. They were endued with power from on high. They began to speak in other tongues, a phenomenon that they could not create themselves. They were doing something that was not natural.

Now, Peter has an anointing. He has been empowered by the Holy Spirit. He witnesses this as an act of God, but the people thought the disciples were drunk. That's when Peters steps in and properly interprets the situation — something he was unable to do a couple of weeks before at Jesus' trial. Peter says, "For these men are not drunk, as you suppose, for it is only the third hour of the day; but this is what was spoken of through the prophet Joel" (Acts 2:15-16). This discernment is infused into Peter by the Holy Spirit. Peter witnesses an act of God and explains what is happening. In a sense, Peter is now witnessing.

Witnessing the Inbreaking of God

As we read through the first three chapters of Acts, we find thousands of people getting saved. Peter witnesses an inbreaking of God and then tells the onlookers what is happening. Mission is more than having our apologetics correct or having our testimonies written out right. Mission is about empowerment. We cannot talk about breaking into the worlds of Islam and Buddhism and Hinduism with simply high-powered apologetics.

At a seminar I was attending, a lady came up to me to share her story about how she witnessed the inbreaking of God in the lives of some people who were lost. This woman, we'll call her Cheryl, moved to Salt Lake City, Utah, with her husband to plant a church. And like most church planters, Cheryl began looking for a new hairdresser. *(Is that what all church planters do?)* She picked a hair salon and made an appointment. During Cheryl's visit to the hair salon, the hairdresser began asking her about why she had moved to Salt Lake City. And in this moment, Cheryl seized the opportunity to share what God was doing in her life: she told the hairdresser they moved to Salt Lake City to plant a church.

Upon the response of the hairdresser, Cheryl began to sense that she was witnessing an inbreaking of God into this woman's life. The hairdresser curiously offered an opportunity to Cheryl, saying, "Well, I'm about to get married, and my boyfriend is a Mormon. I'm not sure how this is going to shape up." Cheryl then followed the Holy Spirit's leading and shared her faith with the hairdresser. Not long after that encounter, Cheryl ended up leading her hairdresser to Christ — along with her hairdresser's boyfriend — and they became part of the core team of the church plant.

Was Cheryl on "hair dresser" evangelism? Or was she out among the stop signs of life and witnessed an inbreaking of missional God? Who was doing what? Who was chasing who? It is missional God who set out on a journey to reach the heart of mankind. A woman in Salt Lake City encounters Cheryl filled with the Holy Spirit; willing to seize the moment, Cheryl gets to witness the actions of God in the heart of the woman.

As Christians, if we will keep our heads low and our hearts filled with expectation, we will be witnesses of God everywhere we venture. To my fellow mission zealots, it's not as though plane rides and languages will help us break into the heart of God. A simple heart bent on listening to what the Father is doing, and open to sharing what He is doing in our own lives, will allow us to be used by God time and time again.

Mission is a spiritual enterprise where we walk in relationship with God. Without the power of the Holy Spirit, we cannot do the work of the Father. We can do many natural things, but we cannot do many things that make a lasting difference.

Witnessing God's Power

In the mid 1980s, my wife and I moved to Santiago, Chile, to plant a church. We knew only a couple of people and had very little cross-cultural training. We were not equipped in our training to accomplish what we had set out to do. But God is gracious and sometimes chooses to show His power through our humble efforts.

Not long after arriving in Santiago, we met a lady named Sonia — whom we never would have found with all of my missiological strategy. My wife and I wanted to learn the Spanish language, contextualize our ministry, and learn the reality of the Chilean culture there in the 1980s. We wanted to do all the background things we could do. We prayed and fasted, and held prayer vigils. We did all the things we knew to do right.

But Sonia came to us — she had her own problems — yet was a God-fearer. As she entered into our lives, I remembered the story of how Paul went down to the river and met Lydia in Acts 16. Paul meets Lydia and has a God encounter with her, causes a riot, and then goes to jail. If you want to use that as a missiological strategy, you've got to meet a woman, cause a riot, and get thrown in jail. In this case, thankfully, God does not always work the same way twice.

As our church was beginning to grow in 1985, we could see the hand of the Lord on our church plant. The growth was a direct result of God working through the hearts of the people in our church, completely distinct from our missiological strategy. And Sonia was a main reason our church began to grow. She was a gatherer. She naturally supernaturally saw the Lord work every day, working in an open marketplace, selling goods to hundreds. Nearly every day, Sonia had God-encounters with people and began inviting them to church and small groups. Over the years, she won scores of people to Christ and discipled them. Her influence on people and impact in the community was probably what solidified that church and our planting of it. At the writing of this book, the church has reproduced itself several times, no doubt because of the tremendous role Sonia played in listening to God and being obedient.[1]

Did I have anything to do with this? I was merely a witness to the inbreaking of God in our little community in Santiago. All I had to do was witness the acts of God and explain what was happening as we went. It was an outpouring of God that can only be explained through the sovereignty of His nature. And I was happy to participate.

This is the "God factor." In your life, there will be things that you did not orchestrate. In fact, you may have had nothing to do with it except be present. But you have eyes to see God doing things and ears to hear His voice. That is the whole joy of walking with God and being a witness of God instead of just trying to witness about Him.

Returning to Acts 16, we see Paul and Silas imprisoned. And this isn't a jail cell with two cots and a simple stone floor. It's a dark, dingy, stark place. Nevertheless, Paul and Silas were praying and singing and worshiping God. The scripture says nothing about them sharing the Gospel with the other inmates. But the other prisoners were just taking it in.

In the middle of Paul and Silas' a cappella worship set, there was an earthquake and we see an inbreaking of God.

As the jailor watched all the doors fly open and knew the inmates would soon escape into the night, he knew he faced certain death from his superiors — so he prepared to kill himself. But Paul knew he was witnessing the acts of God, saw the jailor about to commit suicide, and said, "Do not harm yourself, for we are all here!" (vs. 28). This was clearly the inbreaking of God. This is God the Father, relentlessly pursuing the heart of this jailor and relentlessly pursuing the heart of these prisoners. God had some of His men locked up; the earth trembled; the prison door opened; and Paul, refreshed in the worship service, saw it as an opportunity to share the Good News. He witnessed the power of God. He then told the jailor to believe it, because this was God.

Now, you and I may not see the earth quake, but the Lord is doing a lot more around us than we commonly think. He is at work ministering. Paul witnessed the action of God and then explained it.

God is on a mission, and we all get to participate in His plan. As John Wimber used to say, "Everybody gets to play," which is where we, the common man and the common woman, gain an understanding of what it means to participate in God's mission.

Notes

1. Some of this material was developed through long conversations with Bob Fulton.

Chapter Six

JOE FIFTH PEW

Our call to participate
in what God is doing

If you wait for the perfect moment
when all is safe and assured, it may never arrive.
— Maurice Chevalier

OVER THE LAST SEVERAL YEARS, a young man (we'll call him Joe) from my church in Maine has taken part of his vacation every spring to go on a prayer tour to Spain. Joe was saved in the early 1990s and had, what you might call, a pretty radical salvation. But the interesting thing about this guy is that he's very quiet. You would not consider him a public speaker or a man with a public persona. However, he was very much arrested by the Lord.

Hearing about a group of churches from New England that was going to Spain to pray for direction and vision on planting churches there, Joe volunteered to go. Upon his conversion, Joe had a pretty serious encounter with the Lord that helped him realize his own gifting. The Lord led him to be a part of this prayer tour and Joe obeyed without hesitation. Upon returning from his second trip, he came to my office and said, "We don't pray for Maine and our home church like we do for Spain. We pray with passion and intercede for Spain, but we don't do it for our own church."

I was intrigued by his observations and aggressiveness in the conversation. Joe said the Lord laid it on his heart to pray for our church. He wanted to know if it would be all right if he started a Friday night gathering to pray for our area like we did for Spain. I said, "Of course! If that's what the Lord has laid on your heart, then go ahead and do it."

Then Joe dropped a bomb. He said, "I think we're supposed to pray all night long." I looked at him with the typical reaction of a pastor who was out five or six nights a week already. I said, "I have one question for you: do I have to come?" He assured me that I did not and said, "I'm going to start recruiting in the church." I began to wonder to myself how Joe was going to do this when he's not very outgoing and finds it difficult to strike up conversations with strangers. Joe continued to assure me this was something the Lord laid on his heart. It didn't take long before I realized God had indeed laid something on Joe's heart. He quickly gathered some people together; they began an all-night prayer vigil once a week, praying for our church, our city, and our state, as well as the nation of Spain.

Joe has never been to seminary or Bible school. He was a fairly new Christian when he began going to Spain and came back with the burden for an all-night prayer vigil — and he knew the Father was doing this with him. Joe knew that with his "knower." He became very committed to praying and interceding for our church. In the past several years, Joe has attended almost every spring prayer trip to Spain, paying his own way and taking his vacation to pray for that country. He's not what we would consider a professional missionary. He's who I would call "Joe Fifth Pew."

Joe represents men and women around the world who work hard for their money and hold down a good job, yet see themselves very much involved with the advancement of the Kingdom of God. In Genesis, we saw God set out on a mission mankind. But throughout the Word of God and over the expanse of time, God has always used ordinary people.

As you look at people who God has used through the ages, the further we get from them in history, the greater heroes we make of them. We look at them with reverence and awe; we write books about them; we quote their words. But in their own eyes and the eyes of their contemporaries, they probably thought they were common people.

I don't believe St. Patrick had any idea we would be talking about him today in the 21st century. He knew that he was just a young man from England who had been taken captive and carried to Ireland, but eventually became the patron saint of Ireland. I don't think he thought, "Someday I'll be famous because of what I've done." He was actually referred to as the "green martyr" because he never returned to England once he left. During his day, he surely didn't think of himself as a big person in the history of Christianity.

Francis of Assisi was a simple man who took a vow of poverty. He loved God and everyone around him. Was he big in his own eyes? Absolutely not. Was he big in the eyes of his contemporaries? Not a chance. These men and women who have become marked people in church history were not only small in their own eyes, but they were probably foolish to other people for living the lives that they lived.

Joe represents the person who wants to be spent by God. I don't remember whom I heard say it first, but one of my favorite sayings is this: "I'm a nickel in the pocket of the Lord, and He can spend me any way He wants."

We need to understand that Joe Fifth Pew or Mary Tenth Row in ABC Church around the world is a missional person. Whether they have a call to go to another country and speak another language, or whether they have a seminary graduate degree or do not have a seminary graduate degree, the fact of the matter is this: if someone is walking with God, he is missional and purposeful in his intent to reach out and touch the heart of all mankind.

Therefore, if anyone has a relationship with God, he is a missional person without having to take that on in a professional manner. Whether your hand grips a hammer, grips a stethoscope, grips a wrench, or pushes a pencil, you may see yourself as a common man or a common woman who wants to grow in your relationship with God; but you're more than likely one of those hidden heroes of the faith. It's germane to the movement that I am affiliated with. Our genetic code says, "Everybody gets to play."

In your desire to reach the world, remember this: you do not have to be a professional missionary—you have to be a lover of God. It doesn't matter what you do for vocation.

Everywhere you go during the day, everything you do during the day, you are a missional person.

Wimpy Wheat Thresher to Mighty Hero

When our story begins, we find our main character, Gideon, trembling with fear in a wine vat, well out of view from the mighty Midianites. Gideon is threshing wheat in the most unlikely of places because he fears his enemies might storm down the mountain at any moment and steal away his precious crop. And then an angel of the Lord comes to Gideon and says this: "The Lord is with you, O valiant warrior!" (Judges 6:12). At no point, thus far, do we get the impression that Gideon is a valiant warrior. In fact, the impression we get is that he's a gutless wimp.

But here is an ordinary guy getting drafted into God's service. Who would have seen this coming? While we know Gideon was pretty good at threshing wheat, we have no idea whether he could wield a sword. If he could, he probably wasn't very impressive in his swordsmanship. Yet, God was using Gideon to set the stage for an amazing victory over these people who thrived off tormenting the Israelites.

Gideon was a Joe Fifth Pew. There was nothing extraordinary about him. Neither his physique nor his courage leads us to believe that this man could lead the charge against the massive and powerful army of the Midianites. But after Gideon finally answered God's call on his life to participate in what God wanted to do through him, God used him in the most peculiar, yet powerful way. Gideon and his band of 300 men squashed an army of thousands with trumpets, candles, and clay pots!

What does that have to do with us and the world of mission? Well, we don't have to be trained or professional to accomplish what God wants to do through our lives; however, sometimes God may want us to be trained and work in the professional level of mission. But the point is, just like neither my friend Joe nor Gideon had formal training in the area of missions, God used both of them in powerful ways to impact different situations.

God's desire is to use you, as well, to impact the world in which you live. He is calling you to participate in a mission to reach the world around you. It may look different for each of you, but the call is undeniable. God's people are missional in nature because their creator is.

Getting Involved in Missions

While there may not be a tug on your heart to pack up your belongings and move to Africa or the Middle East as a missionary, you are called to be missional in purpose due to your relationship with God. And as missional people serving God as a body, we find that the local church is the basis from which we can all get involved in mission.

After Paul returned from a lengthy mission trip, Luke shows us in Acts 14 that the sending "agency" for Paul was the local church. "From there they sailed to Antioch, from which they had been commended to the grace of God for the work that they had accomplished. When they had arrived and gathered the church together, they began to report all things that God had done with them and how He had opened a door of faith to the Gentiles" (Acts 14:26-27). Paul wanted to let his supporters know what God was doing abroad.

In his book, *What is Mission? Theological Exploration*, Andrew Kirk explains the importance of local church involvement in missions:

> *Mission is so much at the heart of the church's life that, rather than think of it as one aspect of its existence, it is better to think of it as defining its essence. The church is by nature missionary to the extent that if it ceases to be missionary, it has not just failed in one of its tasks; it has ceased being the church. Thus, the church's self understanding and sense of identity (its ecclesiology) is inherently bound up in its call to share and live out the Gospel of Jesus Christ to the ends of the earth and the end of time.*

So, how can you be missional? Living every day in the routine of life with eyes wide open and a heart full of expectancy. To be missional is not going to another destination. One can be missional in the neighborhood. You can find mission in the nations, but don't limit yourself solely to crossing geographical barriers.

How Can You Be Missional in Your Church

1. **Short-term mission trips.** Not only do short-term mission trips invigorate you spiritually in terms of sharing your faith, they also can energize the missionaries you are aiding. Short-term trips are extremely beneficial in the context of helping church planting movements. Don't balk at an opportunity to participate in a trip of this nature.

In 1974, I had been a Christian for the grand sum of four months and I found myself in the country of Brazil sharing what the Lord had shown me. I had very little training. As a matter of fact, I had no training at all. All I could do was share the story of what God had done in my life. I had no idea that God was beginning to mold me into the man I was to be for my whole life.

People ask me when I received my "call" to the nations. I don't feel like I ever did. Most times, I feel like I got ambushed. That trip in 1974 set into motion an adventure that is beyond description. But I am talking about the adventure with missional God.

Early in my first few trips, I realized God was always bringing us into situations He had prepared ahead of time. And it set me on a course in life that stimulated my sense of expectancy, satisfying my desire to walk with the Lord. A way to get involved with missions is to consider going on a short-term trip to sow the seeds for desire of expectancy in your life.

2. **Prayer tours or prayer walks.** You don't even have to know another language to participate in a trip like this. Just

being a participant in laying the groundwork for prayer covering for the people who will be working in a certain area is of great importance. Prayer is a large part of God's mission.

Though participation in a venture of this magnitude may seem like an overwhelming task, ask yourself a simple question: can I pray? The story I told earlier about Joe and his involvement in praying for future churches in Spain demonstrates that anyone can do this. On the teams that we have sent to Spain, none of them are comprised of famous people. They are made up of common people who take their vacation time and raise the money to go and pray through those countries and cities. As a result, we have a few church plants that are growing in Spain that probably would not have happened if these people had not been praying. I suspect these people would not have had a place on many mission agencies' list defining what a missionary is. But they could pray, so they went.

3. **Prayer groups for targeted areas.** Whenever God begins to move on the heart of a local church for a certain area, a groundwork of prayer must be laid, much like that of going overseas and planting churches. Along the same lines as those groups, you can form prayer groups for areas in your city that you desire to reach.

In the early 1980s, I gathered early each morning with a group of my fellow Bible college students to march around the courtyard traffic circle for about an hour — praying for the people of the nations and the languages we would have to learn upon graduation because we believed God was going to thrust us out all over the globe. This commitment to prayer took place in the harsh cold of New England winters. Following our time together, we would gather in the cafeteria, grab a cup of coffee, and talk about the direction we felt God was moving in our lives. Week after week, we walked around that circle asking God for favor, asking God to raise up churches in lands that had so few.

What were we doing? We always pictured it as laying railroad tracks, like those men and women who worked their way across the United States, connecting the east with the west by pounding rail ties into the ground one at a time. The trains could only go as far as the tracks had been laid. That's how we imagined what we were doing. Now, as I look back almost a quarter of a century later, many of us who walked in that circle have literally been spread around the globe. That's why I'm so convinced that paving the way with prayer really is the battle. We were not yet graduates. We were not ordained. In fact, we were quite naïve. But because we asked, God allowed us to walk out some of His mission around the world.

However, we must remember that we do not need to find purpose for prayer solely in countries abroad. We can even find it in our own backyard.

In 1993 I gathered weekly at an overlook on the eastern side of Portland, Maine, with a group of people committed to prayer for our city. It also was, in a sense, a courtyard of a school. Meeting there at 6 o'clock in the morning each

Wednesday, we would peer out across the city, looking over Back Bay and across the downtown section, into the outlying communities. We asked God over and over to raise up a community of people who would be "lovers of God and rescuers of men." We were a small group of people, but we knew the train could only go as far as the tracks were laid. At the writing of this book, those few people have grown into many hundreds. And the process of planting many congregations from that one has begun. Again, a train can only go as far as the tracks will allow it to go.

4. **Supporting the work financially.** In order to afford a missionary the opportunity to pour his or her heart and soul into reaching the people group they are involved with, they need finances. What an amazing opportunity you have as a believer to partner with missionaries in this way. It excites me to no end to know that I can invest in the advancement of God's Kingdom. And if you draw a paycheck, that same opportunity is available to you.

While I am now in the position to be able to invest in the lives of those God has called to other countries, there was a time when I was the one living in a country far from home, hoping God would stir people's hearts to invest in what He was doing where I lived. How people can really make a difference became a reality for me while living in Chile.

One afternoon I received a phone call from a young man in the United States, telling me he wanted to come and work with us. I thought the first thing I should ask him was his name. He said he was an engineer by profession and had just graduated from Bible school. So, I invited him to come down and visit just to see if our situation in Chile was something that he wanted to join. Upon his arrival, I remember thinking this young man was pretty intense and was ready to get started almost the moment he stepped off the plane. What unfolded was one of the sweetest stories I know in mission support.

After he went out and landed a job in Chile, he said he felt the way he could support our church the most was to make some money and use that money for the planting of churches. Working as an engineer, he lived off the most minimal part of his salary that he could and gave the rest to help the Kingdom grow.

At one of our prayer services, he was face down on the ground in prayer and I noticed the poor condition of his shoes. When I told him to go buy some more shoes, he explained that he would have to wait until his next paycheck. He held nothing back.

For a number of years, he lived this way — donating the lion's share of his income for events, training, and, eventually, multiplication of our church. He is one of my heroes. He has never written a book or put his story on tape, but he used the resources he had. A man from India once told me it really doesn't matter how much money you have, but only what you do with what you have. A little is a lot when it is given to the Lord. It sounds trite, but it's a Kingdom principle. Seed is powerful when it is surrendered to the divine sower.

5. **Tent-making opportunities.** Have you ever thought that the work skills you possess could enable you access to another country where you could share the Gospel? This type of mission work is often referred to as "tent making" because it was how Paul earned some of his support on the mission field. "And because [Paul] was of the same trade, he stayed with them and they were working, for by trade they were tent-makers" (Acts 18:3).

As he entered his short-term mission trip, Matt never thought his job as a computer technology expert could lead him to the mission field on a more long-term basis. However, during one of Matt's conversations with a missionary during a short-term mission trip, he realized that his skills could be used on the mission field — and were desperately needed. At the writing of this book, Matt resides in Switzerland, serving as a missionary through his skills as a computer technology expert.

In many countries that were once part of the former Soviet bloc, churches are sending "missionaries" there to teach business owners about the concepts of running a business. During this process of sharing knowledge of a trade, the people begin asking questions and the opportunity to share the Gospel truth inevitably arises. These men and women who go to share their business knowledge are not the typical missionary types, but they are participating in God's mission by using their talents in a different way.

6. **Local outreaches.** Throughout the years, I have met

many people who have declared openly their fear about sharing their faith with others. Yet when it comes to getting involved in local outreaches, they jump at the opportunity. They may be too timid to talk, but not too timid to demonstrate the love of Christ in a practical way.

Steve Sjogren, the founding pastor of the Vineyard Church in Cincinnati, has explained the "conspiracy of kindness." He has encouraged the people of the church to express kindness, even if they are too scared to share. Sjogren's ideas for local outreaches are simple (i.e., free car washes, giving away sodas on a hot day, giving out smoke detector batteries).

Whether it is a local outreach with low risk or an outreach to a particular people group in a city near you, or a country far away, you can be missional without being a professional missionary. Missional God is at work and you can witness to His works everywhere you go.

When it comes to the local outreaches in your church, building inroads within your community is missional. Lay the tracks right in your neighborhood. Do not bypass the neighborhood while only thinking of the nations. At the same time, don't think only of your neighborhood. It isn't either-or; it's both-and. We need to find every opportunity we can. We walk with a missional God who is on the relentless pursuit of the human heart.

Chapter Seven

NEIGHBORHOODS TO THE NATIONS

Witnessing the acts of God wherever we go

*The highest destiny of the individual
is to serve rather than to rule.*
— Albert Einstein

MEET ALLEN. HE'S A NORMAL GUY with a heart for God, yet he defies the stereotype of your typical pastor, especially in the way that he entered the ministry. Faith was always a big part of Allen's life because he was raised in a Christian home. His deep trust in God never took root until after spending four years in the U.S. Army. When he stumbled into a church one random Sunday, he recommitted his life to God — and his wife gave her life to Christ as well. But Allen was far from entering the ministry, or so he thought.

Allen began serving in the church, working with four-year-olds in the preschool and regularly attending a small group. Then he began working with teenagers in the church youth group.

"I was just going about life, trying to figure out what to do, when I went back to radiology school and took a position at the hospital," Allen said. "As life was happening around me, I was approached by my pastor who asked where I was going and where my life was headed. I knowingly told him I felt like God had a call on my life to minister to others."

Not long after that conversation, Allen joined the church staff.

"I didn't set a course for my life to become a pastor," Allen said, "but I know I ended up where I was supposed to be." As he was going through life, Allen recognized God opening doors and nudging him through them. So, he followed God's lead.

When we think about mission, we must realize that it does not have as much to do with location as it does with relationship to a missional God who is always at work. We are a missional people because we are the people of a missional God.

The Truth about "Foreign" Mission

Oftentimes, we hear about "foreign" mission. However, it's only "foreign" to us because we have not been to a certain place or are unfamiliar with a certain culture. I would suggest that we eliminate the word "foreign." I would like to think that our understanding of mission is what we do as we walk through life. Mission, whether performed in the language of your birth or in a language you've learned, or in your native country or in one you have never visited, is simply doing what you see the Father doing. Unfortunately, I've heard it said, "If everything is mission, nothing is mission." I cannot agree with that statement because I believe everything is mission — it's an extension of the love of God and has nothing to do with where we are.

When we look at the word "mission," we cannot put a higher value on one people group over another. Some of my missionary friends would say if you're not reaching Muslims, you're not doing mission. Others would say if you're not running orphanages, you're not doing mission. I'm sure you've heard some people say if you're not reaching the poor, you're not doing mission. But the fact of the matter is you are doing mission with the poor, with the children, with Muslims, Buddhists, or Hindus. Consider Jesus' outlook on missions:

> *"The harvest is plentiful, but the workers are few. Therefore beseech the Lord of the harvest to send out workers into His harvest."*
> — *Matthew 9:37-38*

Jesus told His disciples they needed to pray for more workers to go into the harvest fields. The harvest is awaiting people like you and me to venture across the street, across our city, and across oceans to take the Gospel to people who are waiting to hear it.

Many churches have broken down mission into two categories — "foreign" and "domestic." And while that may help us delineate between witnessing the works of God in our homeland or witnessing the works of God in a distant land, we must understand that we are all involved in mission. People cannot think that mission happens only when they cross over the ocean and learn another language.

Crossing the street or crossing into a neighborhood is as legitimate as crossing into other nations. However, those who are willing only to cross the street and have no consideration for those who speak other languages and live in other cultures need to be challenged. The mission of God is toward the human heart, wherever the human heart may be.

Three Spheres of Spiritual Reality

There are three different spheres of spiritual reality discernable in the world today.

1. Incredible Harvest. In some places in the world today, there is a harvest going on. People are coming to Christ by the bus loads. Wherever you want to preach, wherever you want to plant a church, you can. It's a sovereign work of God in some areas in the sense that there's no explanation why suddenly there is such a strong move of God.

When you look at the numbers and demographics in places like Latin America, Africa, or Asia today, there are thousands of new churches being planted through many denominations. There's not a particular denomination or movement that is leading the way — it's a joint effort by the body of Christ. Such a harvest is occurring that, wherever you put your shovel in the ground, you come up with diamonds.

Africa has seen the most exponential growth over the past century and early into the 21st century. In 1900, there were only eight million professing Christians on the continent of Africa. By 1970, that number had grown to 117 million and then to 347 million by 2000.

In Asia, the spread of Christianity has also been phenomenal, expanding from 20 million on the continent in 1900 to 96 million by 1970. However, the biggest jump occurred between 1970 and the end of the 20th century, as the number of Christians rose to over 300 million.

Latin America has also shared in the growing number of Christians, swelling from 60 million in 1900 to more than 475 million by the end of the 20th century. And the number only continues to rise.[1]

2. Lightly evangelized, lightly churched. There are other places around the globe that are lightly evangelized, lightly churched regions. This would include places like Spain and France. Is it a harvest? No. Is it totally unreached? No. But in that context, there are some churches and some Christian workers. However, it lies in the middle. Recently, a person was telling me about his burden for France and was lamenting how he was having a hard time getting people to buy into his vision because people didn't see it as a harvest field or as a place that is unreached. This missionary felt somewhat illegitimate in his burden because he wasn't going to the Muslim world and he wasn't exactly working in the harvest sphere. But lightly evangelized, lightly churched is a spiritual reality that needs to be addressed.

John, who served a two-year stint in Scotland and planted a church there, became accustomed to the constant devaluing of his mission to a lightly evangelized, lightly churched region. "Some typical responses to where I was going on the mission field were, 'Wow, aren't you lucky?' or 'That must be nice,' or

'You're going to get to play so much golf over there,'" John said. "Even in missionary circles, I sometimes felt like I was looked down upon. People have a hard time believing that people in Scotland haven't heard the Gospel."

During his time in Scotland, John saw the fruit of short-term teams who were available and willing to be used by God for whatever His purposes were. "One group came over and concentrated on doing service projects and working with the people, building relationships," he said. "And about four months later, I met a man who became a Christian through his interaction with that group." Then there were short-term teams who laid out their own agenda for the people. "We had one group just blitz the town and preach on the street corner — and it didn't seem to make a big difference. The people didn't respond because they didn't know them or trust them."

Ministering in a lightly evangelized, lightly churched area requires hard work and, like every time we step out in faith for God, listening to the Holy Spirit. "Places like Scotland (the lightly evangelized, lightly churched) are full of people who think they have this Christian vaccine," John said. "It's incredible. They have been inoculated with Christianity and think that because they grew up in a 'Christian' nation or were baptized in a church, and because it's a part of their culture, they believe they have salvation. What they really have are icons and monuments to saints. And they need a Savior as much as anyone in any area of the world."

3. Unreached People Groups. The third sphere that has received the most attention from the church in recent years is the unreached people groups. These sectors of different cultures have not had missionaries come in and speak to them about the Gospel. Luis Bush, a modern-day missiologist, coined the phrase that most of us are familiar with in our churches: the 10-40 window. And he did a great service to the body of Christ in bringing so much attention to this area.

Ron and his wife, Kara, who are serving as missionaries in Central Asia along with their four daughters, have discovered great joy while sharing the Gospel with Muslims. However, sharing the Good News in an area that either knows nothing about Jesus or only very little about Him — as well as has incorrect assumptions about Christianity and its ties to the Western world — is certainly challenging.

"Generally, people in the West try to avoid talking about politics and religion," said Ron, who is involved in "tent-making" projects in Central Asia. "In conversations with Muslims, those are two of the topics that come up first. Depending on how much pioneering you are doing in reaching into unreached cultures, you may have more hurdles or fewer hurdles. Some people have preconceived notions about Christians, associating Christianity with all Westerners — which is why I simply say I am a follower of Jesus. Other people only know about Jesus as a prophet through the Islamic faith. It can definitely be challenging."

Though the Muslim world is a great harvest awaiting

willing believers to go into that region, Ron says it isn't for everyone. "When I talk with people about going to the Muslim world, I ask them if the call God has placed on their lives to go is stronger than the one He has placed on their lives to stay. We need to look at some of the fields that aren't around the world, but just across the street."

Though Ron and Kara have received a hero's welcome in many places they have been, they understand that it's simply about being where God has asked them to go. "When I share what we're doing and where we're doing it, our stories elicit two kinds of responses: 'I wish I could go do that' or 'I could never do that' One of my heroes is working in inner city America and, in a sense, is in a much more dangerous area than where I minister.

Wherever God calls us, that is where we should be. Mission is about getting a world view that lines up with the way God views the world — and then everything else falls into place. You go after what He calls you to do, and you see it through His eyes."

As we look at these three different spheres of reality, the trouble begins when you say one of these three is more legitimate than the other two. The Lord has seen fit to call laborers into all of those spheres. We say in Maine, "You need to make hay while the sun is still shining." You want a harvest that is now harvestable. But we need people to work in lightly evangelized, lightly churched countries to disciple leaders and train young leaders on the rise. We need people to work in the harvest countries and help with the spiritual awakening. And we need pioneers who are willing to go into very difficult areas and slug away year in and year out. In each one of those spheres, we need to find people who are willing to discover what the Lord is doing.

What Counts in Mission

In Chapter 5 we talked about witnessing the acts of God, which is crucial to our understanding of how we all fit into God's plan of redemption for mankind. No matter what sphere we venture into — whether it is across the street or around the world — missiological strategy, though important, is not the only thing to consider. In and of itself, our strategy of reaching people lacks the necessary power to be effective. What will matter are Christians who know how to walk with the Lord, who have spiritual eyes, who can see what the Lord is doing and hear what the Lord is saying, and are so secure in their Christianity that they will take risks because they believe God is doing something. The empowerment of the Spirit is not just missiological strategy.

Over the past few years, I have read so many different strategies that, sometimes, it is mind-boggling. There is even a book that lists hundreds of strategies to reach the world for Christ. But the reason they are cataloged in a book is because they have not worked. It isn't just a matter of strategy, even though strategy is important. I don't have a problem with forming strategies and planning and addressing different issues; but if we are going to work in our neighborhoods on the way to the nations, we need to understand the field in which we are working — and we need to do this in a spiritual realm with a spiritual dynamic. We need to see what the Father is doing. And the Father loves to show us what He's doing.

Defining the Mission

When we think about the concept of missions solely in terms of going to another country, we miss the point of what missions is about. We have to come to the place where we recognize that when God made His declaration in Genesis 3:15 — the "I will" of God — that He did not think in terms of foreign missions; rather, God thought in terms of redemption for the entire human race. When God reached into the sea of humanity and plucked out Abram, blessing him so the entire world would be blessed, God wasn't making a statement about legitimate mission fields. As missiologist Chuck Van Engen would say, God was simply saying that "mission is on the way."

When Jesus gave the Great Commission, which I like to refer to more as a repetition of what Jesus told us to do rather than a one-time commissioning, He emphasized that as we go into the world, we are to preach the Gospel. Jesus' intention was not to negate the neighborhoods to get to the "mission field." We are to stop along the way and share with whomever God has placed in our path.

In speaking at different churches about mission, pastors sometimes say to me, "I'm not getting involved with what's going on among the nations because I am committed to what He is doing here." That may be a legitimate statement in and of itself, but even though we are committed to our neighborhoods, there is still the issue of all the nations. When we read Genesis 12:3, Isaiah 49:6, or Isaiah 42:6, God talks about being a light to all the nations. In Revelation 5 and 7, there are people from every tribe, tongue, and nation worshiping God. Evidently, somebody had to be crossing linguistic, cultural, and geographical barriers throughout the ages to spread the Gospel.

We cannot forsake one mission field for another. I wish we could come to a day when churches or mission agencies would simply have a commitment to sending people, without legitimizing some fields and delegitimizing others, when missionaries come with a burden to reach certain areas. The mission of the church is to reach the people among the neighborhoods in which we live, and the people who live oceans away in other cultures and speak other languages. God wants no stone left unturned.

Finding God's Direction

So, how do we know exactly what the Lord would have us to do? Is it being a doctor? A lawyer? A teacher? A pastor? A scientist? A policeman? An architect? How are we going to know? Are we going to hear His voice? Are we going to see

His will written in the sky? Over the years, I don't think I have seen anything paralyze more people than trying to discover the will of God. I have watched people wrestle with the mystical will of God, hoping to have it revealed to them, agonizing over whether or not they are in the center of His will.

> *Therefore be careful how you walk, not as unwise men but as wise, making the most of your time, because the days are evil. So then do not be foolish, but understand what the will of the Lord is. And do not get drunk with wine, for that is dissipation, but be filled with the Spirit.* — Ephesians 5:15-18

The whole thought in this passage — redeem the time, make the most of your time, be filled with the Spirit — in essence, is God's will for our lives. I don't want to oversimplify this statement, but Paul explains the will of God as this: be filled with the Spirit.

> *Finally then, brethren, we request and exhort you in the Lord Jesus, that as you received from us instruction as to how you ought to walk and please God (just as you actually do walk), that you excel still more. For you know what commandments we gave you by the authority of the Lord Jesus. For this is the will of God, your sanctification; that is, that*

you abstain from sexual immorality; that each of you know how to possess his own vessel in sanctification and honor, not in lustful passion, like the Gentiles who do not know God. — 1 Thessalonians 4:1-5

I love the simplicity of the beginning of verse 3: "For this is the will of God, your sanctification." Then Paul goes on to explain what he means by that — the will of God is that your life be set apart for Him. Again, it's like being a nickel in the pocket of God and being willing to allow Him to spend you as He pleases. There is a liberty there — permission for God to do with us as He chooses. That's a life set apart. Is that the will of God for us? It absolutely is.

Gerald Sittser, the author of *The Will of God as a Way of Life*, explains his discovery of God's will:

As I struggled with the issue of discovering God's will in light of my own personal uncertainty, intense suffering, and in-depth biblical study, I came to a startling conclusion. The will of God concerns the present more than the future. It deals with our motives as well as our actions. It focuses on the little decisions we make every day even more than the big decisions we make about the future. The only time we really have to know and do

God's will is the present moment. We are to love God with heart, soul, mind, and strength, and we are to love our neighbors as we love ourselves.

Sometimes, we can make God's will so difficult to grasp that we forget that there are simple commands God gives us, enabling us to do His will each day. God is not trying to trick us — He wants us to get it.

> *Rejoice always; pray without ceasing in everything give thanks; for* this is God's will for you *in Christ Jesus.* — 1 Thessalonians 5:16-18

Paul says the will of God is to have a thankful heart. Through the years at missions conferences and pastors conferences, I've heard people talk about the call of God and the will of God. And while people wrestle through ideas of what exactly it is that God wants them to do, they lose sight of the larger picture, which is who God wants them to be. Early in my Christian walk, someone explained to me in a simple way about God's will for my life, telling me that the will of God would be found in the chemistry of who He made me to be, and that His will won't torture me.

As I have studied the Bible over the years, those three passages continue to jump out at me as a major part of understanding what it means to take the Gospel from the neighborhoods to the nations. It is the will of God that I am a thankful person. It is the will of God that I stay filled with the Spirit. It is the will of God that I am set apart to do His bidding.

When you are doing God's will in this context, let me ask you this question: don't you think you will end up where you need to be, doing what you need to do? When we follow God's will each day for our lives, listening to His voice and responding with obedience, we end up where He wants us to be; whether we are in another country as part of a medical mission team or crossing the street in our own community; whether we are learning a language and translating the Bible into other languages for other cultures; whether we are planting a church in our city or in Africa. People will end up where they are supposed to be by being thankful, by being filled with the Spirit, and by having their lives set apart for whatever God would have them to do. I believe we find the will of God in the walk of life.

A Servant's Mission

In Genesis 24, we find an interesting story about Abraham's oldest servant, who is sent out on a mission to find Isaac a wife. The servant wanted to take Isaac along and let him find his own wife among Abraham's relatives, but Abraham insisted that he bring back a wife for Isaac on his own. Distraught, the servant prayed to God: "O Lord, the God of my master Abraham, grant me success today, and show lovingkindness to my master Abraham." Through a series of tests, the servant met Rebekah and recognized her to be the one. Then, the servant made an interesting statement: "Blessed be the Lord, the God of my master Abraham, who has not forsaken His lovingkindness and His truth toward my master; as for me, the Lord has guided me in the way to the house of my master's brothers" (vs. 27).

Proverbs 10:17 says, "He is on the path of life who heeds instruction, but he who forsakes reproof goes astray." Just like Abraham's servant obeyed Abraham's wishes and ventured into a difficult mission, when we obey God and maintain humility in our lives, we are going to be on the pathway of life. If there is a willingness to be set apart for God, we will be in the will of God. If there is a desire to be continually filled with the Spirit, we will be in the will of God. God says it is His will that we are thankful. In being thankful, we are on the path of life because we are heeding instruction.

Abraham's servant found his way because he was walking. He did not have a charismatic experience, even though that can happen. I am not saying that you can't hear those clear voices of direction that tell you exactly where to go. But this man found his way by simply walking in obedience. God led him exactly to the place where he was supposed to be to accomplish his mission.

Many people ask about the will of God as far as it relates to their vocation or the geography of where they should live. However, the question we should be asking is, "How should we live?" The Bible clearly states God's will for our lives. Get those things straight and you will end up where you're supposed to be. Remember, God is on a relentless pursuit for the heart of mankind — and He wants to get you there as urgently as you want to get there. If that is in the neighborhood or on a medical mission team or on a church planting team in another country, then God will put you there. The most important issue is that you're missional in the neighborhoods on the way to the nations.

We now have to consider that we're not just talking about you as an individual, but we're also talking about corporate life. What does this mean not only as a missional person but also belonging to a missional community and the power that we find in the life of the local church?

Notes

1. Source: David B. Barrett & Todd M. Johnson. International Bulletin of Missions Research, 2004.

Chapter Eight

THE GOOD
OF THE WHOLE

The power
found in unity

*You can accomplish anything in life
provided that you do not mind who gets the credit.*
— Harry S. Truman

AS A LEADER, I have constantly sought ways to improve the way in which I lead. Not many people have articulated the ideal team to lead the way George H. Bush did early during his term as president in 1989. I once heard Bush describe his ideal team as one in which he is surrounded with intelligent people who are creative, innovative, and articulate. He wanted to have people who are problem-solvers instead of problem identifiers. He also wanted people to be unafraid to articulate their ideas. Bush said he wanted people to be able to defend their ideas, even in the midst of disagreement or ridicule. However, these people also had to have a willingness to walk out of the room as a team united in purpose, even if their individual ideas were not used in the final decision.

I remember thinking, "That is the kind of team I would like to work with." Teams that are articulate and know how to defend themselves are united in purpose because they think more of the team than of their individual status.

When it comes to reaching the world for Christ, whether it's in our neighborhoods or in the nations, nothing is more important than teamwork. Once we make the conscious decision to be intentional in the way we reach out to people, we discover that it is difficult to do so on our own. As the body of Christ, we are all in this mission together — and we must all participate if we desire to see the maximum impact.

What is God Doing?

When people ask me what I feel the Lord is doing in the big picture, I have always been surprised at the question. The inference from the question is that the Lord is fickle and changing His mind every day. This question is not couched in terms of discovery, as in how God is stirring the hearts of people, but in terms of what the latest move of God is. It is part of the nature of our culture to be fresh and new, cutting edge, pushing the envelope, and avante-garde. We want to be the biggest and the best, the latest and the greatest. We want new revelations, higher thoughts, deeper water.

However, God is doing what He set out to do in Genesis. In one sense, God *has* done what He set out to do. As we see the New Jerusalem in Revelation 21 and 22 where the bride and the groom are together, we know that is accomplished. That is what the Lord is about today. The 21st century church doesn't need another new thing to get occupied with. The 21st century believer and 21st century church simply need to stay the course, walk on the shoulders of those who have gone before us, and do that until. God is relentlessly pursuing the human heart, preparing the people to be His bride. And He will keep doing that until it is a reality.

In desiring to understand missional God and His will for our lives, we need to understand we are not an island unto ourselves.

Lone Ranger Mentality

Finding the will of God for your life as a person is just a portion of the picture. If we approach our Christianity on an individual basis as a Lone Ranger, we will never experience the fullness of what God has for our lives. In God's sovereign plan, He has chosen to operate through the church. Jesus helped set up the structure of the church before He ascended into heaven.

When a person finds his or her place in a church where they are learning to operate in the body of Christ, the power of one person's spiritual gifts is multiplied many times over. Oftentimes, we don't even know the entire inventory of our own gifts, much less our callings and potential contributions to the body of Christ. Then we look in a mirror and feel inadequate for the task at hand. As one person, we look at the task of world evangelism or discipling people and say, "What good could I do by myself?" However, we find more power and effectiveness when we are operating within the body of Christ.

Looking in a mirror while we are alone, we don't see the fullness of who we can become. But when we look in the mirror through the eyes of the body of Christ, we see great potential reflected to us in the power of the whole. For example, maybe you never saw yourself as a teacher, but someone else within the body recognized your gifting in that area and pointed it out to you. With some encouragement, discipleship, and opportunity, you could use your gifting to benefit the entire body.

In order to truly discover who we are and how we fit into the bigger picture, we need the body of Christ to affirm and confirm us — to help us discover who we are and what we are about. If we are an island unto ourselves, we cannot operate in the bigger picture. In the New Testament, the leaders laid hands on and blessed those who were sent out to do the work of the Lord, bearing witness to the gifts the leaders saw stirred up within these commissioned saints. As we take a look at the church itself, we realize how it relates to our faith, understanding that the church is an important part in our growth as believers, and enabling us to figure out what our roles are.

The Role of the Local Church in Missions

As we look at the vast expanse of missions, the local church is the vehicle best equipped for reaching the world in an effective way. In their book, *Changing the Mind of Missions: Where have we gone wrong?*, James Engle and William Dyrness explain the importance of the local church in the process of taking the Gospel around the globe:

> A central theological reality is that the church is uniquely equipped to be the locus of missions because it is essentially missionary by its very nature. This means that the church itself is the missionary reality that God's [sic] sends into the world. It is far more than an institutional source from which funds and mis-

sionaries are sent or agency-developed programs are carried out. Indeed it is both the message and the medium expressing the fullness of the reign of Christ.

As we're talking about missional God, missional people, and the history of this whole concept of understanding what the Lord is doing and being a witness to it, understand that this is in the context of a people, plural, not just the individual. There have been a couple of times I have led mission teams both inside the United States and outside the United States when a person has said to me, "If it's good for the team, it's good for me." Even if these people thought differently about the direction of the team, they were still willing to say, "If this is where the team is going, then this is good enough for me." Now, the people who told me this were not listless "yes men." They were people who were energetic and very creative, full of good ideas. However, they understood the purpose and goal of our mission.

In reflecting upon what we do or where we go as a church to reach the lost, we must understand we have to do it together. A lady in my church once told me that she would find her place in "the good of the whole." In other words, she wanted to know how she could best help the community. That is the type of mentality that makes mission so real. You find an empowerment, a release, a covering, and a protection when you walk with other people in what God has called you to do.

If you're talking about mission as far as crossing linguistic barriers, cultural barriers, or geographic barriers, it is difficult to do that alone. How many casualties are there of individuals who go out by themselves instead of going as a team? They are sitting ducks. I know there are cases where that is the only way the Gospel may reach a certain region. But where it doesn't have to happen, we need to be more responsible. We can't send out a soldier to do the work of a troop, or a troop to do the work of an army.

Church-based mission means that all mission is really based out of the local church and the initiative comes from the church. For so long, churches have abdicated their position of being a missional people. In every way, we want to appreciate and recognize what mission agencies have done over the last century and beyond. But the fact of the matter is the church is the institution called to do the bidding of God. There has been argument over who should be sending people to the global mission field — the mission agencies or the church? Some people say let the professionals send missionaries. Others say let the church send people in a strategic manner. It is a debate in the missiological world. But with the capability that we have within our churches to mobilize people to reach out, we cannot shrug our shoulders and walk away from such a grave responsibility.

The Example of Paul

In studying Paul's ministry, we have a biblical example of

what it means to be sent from a local church. Paul was a member of a local church, not an individual who roamed the world seeking an audience for his message. Through a series of events, Paul was brought into the life of the church in Antioch. He became a part of the leadership team there and was used in a powerful way in the discipleship of the church. But at a time of God's choosing in Acts 13, the Spirit of God came on the leadership team and they sent Paul and Barnabas on a particular missional outreach. Paul was sent from the local church with someone.

Though both Paul and Barnabas went all over their region, they always came back to their local church in Antioch. Paul saw himself as part of a team, part of a church. He stayed connected with that church. He was a local church person. Paul found his place in the good of the whole. He was living in obscurity in Tarsus until he was invited by Barnabas to come into the life of the church in Antioch.

In the context of that church, Paul's place was better defined. As he was sent out and blessed by that church, the full revelation of who Paul was called to be was finally realized.

Reaching the World in Unity with Love

> *"By this all will know that you are My disciples, if you have love for one another."* —
> John 13:35

Jesus explains that the world will not know you are a disciple because of your knowledge or commitment or because of your set apart life, but because you live among a people whom you love. In missions, sometimes the greatest testimony in the neighborhood is the testimony of community itself — the unconditional love of God. That testifies to people. It is a witness to the whole world when they see people loving one another. That's walking as a whole, walking together in the church.

Bob Fulton, the International Coordinator for the Vineyard Movement, once said, "We are committed to outreach out of the local church. The local church is the outreach." That is foundational to impacting our world: the local church has to reach out. Even when the church has abdicated its place and merely taken an offering to support mission, you will find your place in the good of the whole. Synergy is extremely important to being effective in reaching the world with the Gospel.

The Corporate Power of the Church

"Five of you will chase a hundred, and a hundred of you will chase ten thousand, and your enemies will fall before you by the sword."
— Leviticus 26:8

The principle in this passage explains that five can chase 100, and 100 can chase 10,000. It is the idea that there is power when we work corporately. The power of the whole is greater than any individual component. What one horse can pull, two horses can pull faster and with greater ease — and they can do it more effectively than two separate horses pulling alone. They pull more together than individually. This is why it is so important to understand the corporateness of the church.

In practical ways, local church-based mission goes back to the principle of everybody getting to play. A testimony we have seen occurring around us is that many churches have become very committed to their neighborhoods as well as the nations. They have not just sent missionaries to another nation, but they have decided to be committed to the city in which they live. As I have mentioned earlier, there is a group of churches in New England committed to raising up a church planting movement in Spain. There are also others groups of churches working together to plant churches in Cuba. And in both Spain and Cuba, these new churches are working together to plant churches there themselves. These are all synergistic partnerships that came from the idea that we can do more together than we can do by ourselves.

As we find the will of God for our lives, we find it to a greater depth when we find our place in the corporate expression of the local church. I think it is majestic how the Lord has put the body of Christ together. God has placed everybody in the body as it pleases Him (1 Corinthians

12:18). The Lord probably gets a divine chuckle out of having men and women who rub each other the wrong way placed in the same local expression of His body. Though we may wish it otherwise, the church is not made up of people who have personality rapport, but of people who love God. In the same context, just like an individual is going to find a greater expression of God's will in the corporate church, the average church will find a greater expression of God's will when they partner with other churches.

In general, most churches do not have the resources they need to cross linguistic, cultural, and geographical barriers. But if a group of churches bands together and forms a partnership, then the churches can do something that they could not do alone. The same idea that enables us to understand God's will for our lives helps us in our work in the context of mission.

In my years as a missionary, I remember seeing numerous efforts get started in South America. But when the church that was sponsoring the project began going through difficult financial times, they usually pulled support for the missionary These churches had great intentions, but I remember thinking, "Why doesn't a group of churches commit to working together until this project gets going?"

It is a source of pride for a church to say we support 15 different missionaries. But when the reality of it is fleshed out, 15 different people are getting $15 per month. The people in the church are mostly uninvolved in the lives of the missionaries, usually without a clue about how they are doing in the field. Dare I suggest that, instead of a church trying to support 15 different works, that we have 15 churches support one church planting movement project?

Forming Partnerships

Since returning from South America, one of the biggest soap boxes I have climbed on has been that of local church partnerships. I always wondered why churches did not decide to partner together to reach a particular region. Churches have awesome potential sitting in their rows and pews. Leaders should harness energy and resources in order to get people into our neighborhoods as well as the nations around the world.

In 1990 when I moved back to the United States and became affiliated with the Vineyard church movement, I remember traveling around New England and sharing with other local churches about a church planting project in Spain. I explained to them the idea of doing it together, all of us pitching in our time, energy, and money toward raising up churches in that country. We started it together. Over a decade later, it is now happening. It is slowly becoming a reality, but it is happening. This model of churches working together in a partnership has been embraced by churches all over the United States and in other parts of the world.

Some churches with vast amounts of resources are capable of participating in many different efforts on their own. And most of us would applaud that, secretly wishing we had such resources to do the same work in our own church. But the size of the average church across the country does not lend itself to such massive projects worldwide. However, if churches are willing to work together, they can accomplish much more. Instead of a church blowing its own horn and saying, "We have done this" or "We have done that," the church can say, "We have advanced the Gospel with other churches in our area." One church might take care of legal issues. Another church may be the prayer covering for the work, while another church may handle all the communications. One may be responsible for the logistics of travel. One may be responsible for caring for the national leaders in the field when they return on furlough.

This concept of partnership works just as well for reaching our neighborhoods as it does the nations. Instead of an individual church being raised up and using all its resources to plant a church, many churches can plant a church together. In fact, they would probably be more successful doing it that way than each church attempting to plant alone.

In Atlanta, a large Presbyterian church invited both small and large churches in the area to join together to reach their community for Christ, forming a group called "Unite!" Their vision is "to unite churches to pray, serve, and celebrate together so that our community sees our good works, experiences transformation, and glorifies our Father who is in heaven." And the results have been astounding! After all the messages of divisiveness that have been communicated from local churches, there is a new message being communicated by the churches in this area: they are united in the cause of the Christ. The churches involved include various worship expressions and numerous ethnic congregations. And it all came about because a handful of church leaders thought it would be better for the Kingdom if they worked together instead of apart.

Whatever you do, do it with somebody. Embrace the people the Lord has placed around you. Know that you will find your place in the good of the whole.

Chapter Nine

SCREAMING ON INTO ETERNITY

Where we are headed

For now we see in a mirror dimly, but then face to face; now I know in part, but then I will know fully just as I also have been fully known.
— 1 Corinthians 13:12

IT WAS SUCH AN EXCITING DAY when my daughter Jenna, along with her husband Shawn, came up to me while on a mission trip in Juarez, Mexico, and told me they had brought 20 teenagers on the mission trip and a baby! I thought it was foolish of them to bring 20 teens *and* a baby, so I tried to politely tell Jenna that probably wasn't the best idea. Then, she just looked at me with those beautiful eyes of hers and said, "No, daddy, a baby." With that, she patted her tummy and I suddenly caught on — my daughter was expecting her first child.

I remember the tears I cried and the joy that welled up inside of me. Almost immediately I had an instant picture of the first 20 years of her life, remembering the excitement that just blazed through my being. Now she was going to have the opportunity to experience the same thing with her new child — and the baby wasn't even born yet! The baby, whom we have since come to know and love as Marie Janette, still had the whole gestation period to go.

It would be nine months later that we actually got a chance to see this little precious life. Twenty minutes after Marie Janette was born and came screaming into the world, they brought her into the room and you could see a wonderful little life had started. While in the womb, Marie Janette was living, but she was far from the fullness of life that awaited her.

Understanding Eternity

Reflecting on the period of gestation — from conception to birth — helps me come to grips with, and understand with greater depth, the meaning of eternity. Revelation 21:4 has always been a verse that has intrigued me: "And He will wipe away every tear from their eyes; and there will no longer be any death; there will no longer be any mourning, or crying, or pain; the first things have passed away." As John looks into the future, he sees the gestation period for humanity has come to an end. All the "first things" have ended. Just as in Genesis 1 and 2, there was no pain, no tears, no brokenness, no psychiatric hospitals, no AIDS, no abandonment. John clearly sees the beginning of the age to come and the dwelling together of God and His bride. It simply means the gestation period — called the "first things" — had ended.

John realized that our time on earth was not the end; rather, it was the beginning. He understood that we would be screaming into eternity, not limping into the next lifetime.

As we come to the close of this book in our adventure with missional God, I think we have to look at the fact that we are going somewhere. We are not just on this journey trying to be good so God will love us. We are going somewhere.

As people who believe in God and in His Son; as people who believe in the redemption provided to us by the Son of God and His pending second coming, that becomes our North. That is the perspective we take by which we live our lives. What we are doing now prepares us for the age to come.

Many times when you are in the woods, it is easy to get disoriented and lose your North. All the trees look the same. You wonder how you got into the woods or where you will get out, if you even get out at all. But if you are a smart woodsman, you have a compass in your pocket. You pull it out and begin to plot a course that will lead you out of the woods. Knowing where North is helps you navigate through the clutter.

I think many people in the 21st century have lost sight of what their North is. People, whether in the church or out of the church, do not really understand their destiny. Forget living — they are simply trying to survive. What would your reaction be if, after her gestation period, little Marie Janette was born and said, "Wow! What a great life I just lived! That was incredible!" We would say that is ridiculous. She has barely been alive. Well, that is what we should think about our time on earth. That is how we should view our time on this planet. If we really believe what the Bible says about eternity, we should come to the complete realization that life here on earth is just the gestation period. Don't get me wrong — I love life! I am milking it for every moment it is worth. This is not doom and gloom. However, my North is found when what I believe by faith becomes my reality.

"When the Work is Done, We All Go Home"

There are moments when the most profound words come from the mouths of children. I experienced this with my son not long after we had just returned from Brazil on one of our extended stints there as missionaries. During our time on the mission field, our children always loved living wherever we lived, but they also enjoyed our visits back to the United States — Maine in particular. One church invited us to share what was happening and our experiences in Brazil. On our way home from that church in the car, Aaron, who was seven years old at the time, was verbally processing his current reality. This is the way he put it: "Let's see," he began. "First, we lived in a wooden house we built in Maine. Then we lived at a Bible college. And then we lived in Brazil. But we know that our real home is in Heaven. When the work is done, we'll all go home."

Now, that is quite a statement for a seven-year-old. It amazed me and Janet that Aaron grasped the concept that we were pilgrims. And I don't believe it was just because we were missionaries, traveling from place to place. Aaron, who is now the director of a Christian school, had heard enough sermons by age seven to know that this was the reality of life. Not only do the scriptures point to the eternal city north of me, but a comment such as this — even said by a seven-year-old — keeps everything in perspective for me. There is so much more to life than we see.

Over the years, people I have pastored have asked me

what I think about the end times. Am I pre-trib? Post-trib? Pre-millennial? What is going to happen? And when is it going to happen? To all of which I simply answer, "Yes." Seriously, I believe in the end times — they are coming. My eschatology is simple, and it is wrapped up in Jesus' words spoken in Matthew 24:14: "This gospel of the kingdom shall be preached in the whole world for a witness to all the nations, and then the end will come."

I firmly believe in the Parousia, the second appearing of Christ. Yes, that day is coming and I believe that it will usher in the age to come. I am committed to the idea that when the disciples asked Jesus in Matthew 24 when the end would come, He clearly stated it will happen after the "gospel of the kingdom shall be preached in the whole world for a witness to all the nations." In other words, after everybody gets an opportunity to hear of God's love, then the end will come.

While it is the end of this age, it is the beginning of things to come. At the end of this "gestation period" on earth, we will go screaming into eternity. I don't think we have the faculties to fully understand what this means. It boggles my mind when I try to sit down and think about forever and what that translates to in terms of my life. But that's our North. That is where we are headed.

In the end, God's intent will be realized again. The phrase "back to the future" was popularized by a movie by the same title starring Michael J. Fox in the 1980s. Fox played a character who was transported into the past and made it his goal to get "back to the future." He had already been there and desperately wanted to return. That analogy helps me understand this Kingdom principle: as I am going forward, I am returning to what God once gave humanity here on earth. We will have fellowship with God, full and complete intimacy with Him. In searching for our true North, we find it through discovering the love that God has for people. Immediately after the fall of man when we lost what we had, God threw down the gauntlet and said, "I will not quit on the human race." He set into motion a plan that allows us to enter into fellowship with Him and have the close communion that we so desperately desire — and need. And that is worth giving my life for. That helps me see the bigger picture in a powerful way.

If we truly believe what the Bible says, this phrase comes to mind as being the mantra by which we move forward: "If it's worth anything, it's worth everything." That is what God says about us. If people are worth anything, they are worth everything — even the life of My only Son.

What It Means to be Missional People

Let us consider what we have stated throughout this book. We believe God set out on His mission for our benefit, calling us to Himself for His purposes. We are called as His people. We walk with Him, not ahead or behind. What He is up to, we are to be up to. When you look through the scope of the last several thousand years, there is a clear understanding that we walk on the shoulders of faithful men and women. They have taken the story of Jesus around the globe, and we are charged to do the same. What were they doing as they were going? They were discovering the acts of God. It was not them taking God to the nations and to people groups around the world. These were wanderers in the best sense of the word. They were on a journey with God, discovering what He was doing among the people of the earth.

We have said there is no more important thing than discovering what the Father is doing and then going ahead and doing it with Him. It isn't a matter of mission activitism — it is a matter of walking out our life with God, developing spiritual eyes to see and ears to hear what the Father is doing. In that discovery, we find His mission; we realize what He is doing. We witness His activity, and we say, "This is that."

One of the motives of this book has been to communicate with the body of Christ that everybody gets to do this. Missional God working through a missional people is something that involves everybody. There's no special group. There's no elite. There's no professionalism. This is about passion. You are able.

Are you willing?

As we walk with missional God, we have now come to the full conviction that it is not about crossing linguistic and cultural barriers; rather, it is about walking in our neighborhoods on our way to the nations, whether those nations live around us in the ethnic make-up of our cities, or across the oceans in different countries. Where we are, we are walking with missional God, participating in His mission.

As you, the reader of this book, think about how the Lord is working around you, ask Him, "What are You doing? What are You doing in my everyday life?" Is God working in the life of your mechanic? Is He at work in the life of your professor? Is He moving in the heart of your boss? Is He stirring the soul of your neighbor across the street? As you walk, go forward expecting God to reveal to you what He is doing. Look for it daily. The scripture clearly teaches us that the Father is always at work. As you walk with missional God, remember that you are not alone. He is already at work and He wants you to join Him.

In setting out on your walk with missional God, remember that you walk with missional people, in a synergistic effort with many. The power of the whole is greater than any individual component. Remember that you are walking toward a day when there will be no more pain, no more tears. The consummation of the Kingdom of God becomes a reality.

I believe we are nearing the end of gestation. I look forward to the day that faith becomes sight and we go screaming into eternity. But until then we must stay the course. We must remember where our true North is.

Everywhere you go, the Father is present and the Father is always working — and He loves to show you what He is doing. You are a missional person if you walk with God. Ask for the eyes and ears to see and hear. Hang on and enjoy the ride!

Chapter Ten

PROCLAMATION BY DEMONSTRATION

How we tell
when we show

*Truly I say to you, to the extent that you
did it to one of these brothers of Mine,
even the least of them, you did it to Me.*
— Matthew 25:40

AS THE CHURCH SOLDIERS on into the twenty-first century, capturing God's heart for others has begun to take on a "new" shape — a shape that is, in fact, centuries old. How the church in the U.S. drifted away from its call to *be* Jesus to the world is a topic discussed in plenty of books these days. Regardless of why this happened, a monumental shift is taking place. Telling people about Jesus is no longer enough: we need to show them Jesus.

Katie Davis personifies this shift, sharing her incredible story in *Kisses from Katie*. As a 19-year-old girl growing up in Tennessee, Katie grew up going to church in a culture fixated on the pursuit of the American dream. *Be a good girl. Attend church. Talk about your faith with your friends.* But, after graduating from high school, she went to Uganda where Jesus "wrecked" her life. It wasn't enough just to talk about it any more.

She explains:

"Slowly but surely I began to realize the truth: I had loved and admired and worshiped Jesus without doing what He said. This recognition didn't happen overnight; in fact I believe it was happening in my heart long before I even knew it. ... It was happening in so many ways, and I couldn't deny it. I wanted to actually *do* what Jesus said."

The rest of Katie's story is a cold-water wake-up call to anyone feeling that they are mired in mediocrity when it comes to their faith. Eventually, she moved to Uganda and started adopting kids, serving as their mother, educator and provider. Fourteen, to be exact. She's surely not done either.

Demonstration's Proclamation

As we study Jesus' life, we see Him as a relentless proclaimer of Good News. Every village He visited, every mountainside He spoke from, every encounter He had — they all share the incredible truth of the Gospel: God loves us and He's come to set us free.

But Jesus didn't restrict His proclamations of the truth to mere words. He relied on His actions, too. Jesus didn't wait until His crucifixion and resurrection to show God's love and fulfill the prophesy of the Old Testament. Everywhere Jesus went He healed people. He cast out demons. He healed the sick. He washed dirty feet.

For so long, we have considered the proclamation of the Gospel as nothing more than storytelling. We have encouraged people to get a grasp of their testimony so that they can share it at a moment's notice. Seminars and conferences were built around the idea of learning how to share your faith so that others would be persuaded to make a decision to follow Christ. As the culture grew more sensitive to open conversations about God, the focus of these seminars shifted to how we could engage people in conversation that would bring up God more naturally.

While it is important to understand what you believe, why you believe it, and be able to communicate it clearly, people watch what you do more than what you say. The most convincing argument to follow Christ that's ever been made pales in comparison to being the hands and feet of Jesus. Despite our inclination to go and tell, Jesus calls us to proclaim the Gospel with our actions as well.

Here's what Jesus said:

> "Then the King will say to those on His right, 'Come, you who are blessed of My Father, inherit the kingdom prepared for you from the foundation of the world. For I was hungry, and you gave Me *something* to eat; I was thirsty, and you gave Me *something* to drink; I was a stranger, and you invited Me in; naked, and you clothed Me; I was sick, and you visited Me; I was in prison, and you came to Me.' Then the righteous will answer Him, 'Lord, when did we see You hungry, and feed You, or thirsty, and give You *something* to drink? And when did we see You a stranger, and invite You in, or naked, and clothe You? When did we see You sick, or in prison, and come to You?' The King will an-

swer and say to them, 'Truly I say to you, to the extent that you did it to one of these brothers of Mine, *even* the least *of them*, you did it to Me.'" — Matthew 25:34-40

Embracing Social Justice

Many Christians have grown leery of the phrase "social justice," fearing that it ascribes to the belief that works are more important than faith. But when God captures our hearts, we want to do things in His name. We can't ignore the broken and crumbling world around us; such brokenness compels us to do something.

In recent history, the church has been shifting, broadening its mission to include the pursuit of social justice. When we think of the proclamation of the Gospel, it must include being merciful and compassionate to the poor, standing up for those who can't stand up for stand for themselves, speaking up for those who can't speak up for themselves, defending those who can't defend themselves. The church is rediscovering these issues and experiencing an awakening.

It's not a contrived effort to get our tentacles into more sectors of society; rather, it's a return to the heart of the Gospel. It's recognizing that God's compassion extends far beyond the mere quest for our love and into the desire to make us whole again, no matter what state of brokenness we're in.

What Social Justice Looks Like

Social justice encompasses a gamut of issues like the environment and world hunger, which the church is being forced to reckon with. In what ways do we need to become better stewards of the world God has entrusted us with? And how is God calling us to combat world hunger and the devastating global effects of starvation on people and cultures? We're even struggling with the wretched issue of human trafficking. The idea that people are bought and sold as objects—modern day slavery—is revolting on every level. Yet, the church can no longer stand on the sidelines. Instead, the church must lead the charge and take every opportunity to show the world the compassion and the love of Christ.

Sometimes social justice isn't wrapped up in high profile ministries like freeing sex slaves from human trafficking or stamping out hunger in impoverished nations. It can also look like fifty men and women changing oil on a Saturday morning.

Changing oil might seem like an odd way to proclaim the Gospel and demonstrate God's love for others, but it isn't really. For single moms trying to stretch every dime they have, the choice between winterizing their automobile or purchasing food for a week takes little time to consider—hunger always takes precedence.

So, we decided that single moms in our community wouldn't have to wrestle with that dilemma—they could have a winterized car *and* food. And so every fall, between sixty and seventy men and women at the church volunteer their time to winterize these cars for single moms and host them for breakfast. God always comes up in the conversation.

As God's relentless pursuit results in taking your heart captive, the truth becomes clearer and clearer. God is interested in more than just a simple affirmation that we love Him and that we're following Him. He's also interested in us sharing His love with others in meaningful and powerful ways — ways that show He's in love with His sons and daughters.

SMALL GROUP DISCUSSION

Chapter One: Missional God

Central truth
God began the relentless pursuit of the human heart immediately after sin entered the world.

Text
Genesis 1-3

Questions
1. Whenever you have suffered loss in your past, how have
you responded? Was there any way you could recover any of
your loss? If so, what did you do about it?

2. According to God's intent for humanity, why do we seem
to have an innate desire for community?

3. In what ways have you seen community and intimacy
work together in your life?

4. How have you seen missional God at work in your own
life?

Chapter Two: Missional People

Central truth
When we become God's people, we take on His mission by participating in what He is doing.

Text
Genesis 12:1-3

Questions
1. In what ways have you embraced the passions of God for your own life?

2. What expectations have you had for God to work in your life? What happened when those expectations were filled?

3. How have you become a missional person since making the decision to follow God?

4. Share a recent "inbreaking" of God into your normal, everyday life in the past month.

Chapter Three: Standing on Their Shoulders

Central truth

As participants in God's mission, we are standing on the shoulders of men and women who have gone before us to prepare the way for God's message to reach the heart of humanity.

Text

1 Thessalonians 5:11-22

Questions

1. In your own experiences, how have you moved forward in life because of another person who blazed the trail ahead of you?

2. Tell about a time in your life when you went through a period of difficulty to see, only later, that it was God who led you there for a purpose.

3. How has God used people in ways, unbeknownst to them, to encourage you in your faith?

4. How can you respond to God when you are experiencing a difficult situation in your life?

Chapter Four: Discovering God at Work

Central truth

The essence of mission is discovering what God is doing and joining Him.

Text

John 5:16-20

Questions

1. What has been your experience in the past when you have tried to do anything for God on your own strength?

2. How has your desire to see God at work in and around your life increased your expectancy to see Him work?

3. What can you do each day to commit yourself to following the leading of the Holy Spirit?

4. How does spending time alone with God directly affect your ability to see what He is doing?

Chapter Five: Witnessing Versus Being a Witness

Central truth

As we witness the power of God on a regular basis, our story not only becomes more powerful, but it openly demonstrates God's love in an undeniable way.

Text

Acts 4:32-35

Questions

1. What is the difference between witnessing versus being a witness?

2. How have you witnessed the inbreaking of God in your life? In the lives of others?

3. What opportunities have you taken to get involved with what God is doing around you?

4. How can you live naturally supernaturally?

Chapter Six: Joe Fifth Pew

Central truth
God wants to use everyone — everyone is qualified to be used by Him.

Text
Judges 6-7

Questions
1. Have you ever felt any kind of call on your life to serve God? Describe what that call was like?

2. What has been your experience while on an outreach, whether in your community or abroad? What did God teach you through that experience?

3. In what ways have you and your church reached out to the community in creative ways? What are some other ways you can creatively connect with people in your community?

4. How has prayer prepared you before you have reached out to your local community?

Chapter Seven: Neighborhood to the Nations

Central truth

Mission opportunities are all around us — and we must never forsake the neighborhoods on our way to the nations.

Text

Matthew 9:37-38

Questions

1. What type of value have you placed on people in certain parts of the world over others? Does your value system align with God's value toward people?

2. According to this chapter, what counts the most in mission? Why?

3. How can we define God's mission?

4. What are three things that the Bible tells us is God's will for our lives? How does this help us live?

Chapter Eight: The Good of the Whole

Central truth

When we don't care what church or ministry gets the credit, the body of Christ can advance God's Kingdom in powerful ways.

Text

Romans 12:3-8

Questions

1. How does being part of the body of Christ help us grow? How does it help us advance God's Kingdom?

2. How does working together not only within our local church but with other churches strengthen the body?

3. What message does a body of believers unified in purpose send to the world?

4. How can you partner with other local churches in your community?

Chapter Nine: Screaming On into Eternity

Central truth
As we embrace God's mission, we must also embrace His eternal perspective, realizing that our life on earth is just a small piece in God's plan for us.

Text
Revelation 21:1-8

Questions
1. How does taking on an eternal perspective inspire you to join in God's mission?

2. After reading this book, what does it meant to you to be a missional person?

3. What steps can you take to develop your spiritual eyes and ears?

4. How are you going to respond when you see the Father doing something around you? How do you think your response will change the way you view life?

Chapter Ten: Proclamation by Demonstration

Central truth

In our changing culture, when it comes to sharing the love of Christ and the Gospel message what we do is just as important—if not more so—than what we say.

Text

Matthew 25:34-40

Questions

1. What are some ways that you can show others the love of Christ?

2. In what ways have you encountered people who were resistant to the Gospel when you shared your faith with them?

3. How have you seen barriers broken down through simple acts of kindness?

4. What are some effective ways you've been able to share your faith in a way that piques people's curiosity and leads to a conversation about faith?

About the Authors

PHIL STROUT is a committed leader and communicator in the 21st century church. He brings over thirty-five years of experience in the areas of church planting and cross-cultural missions. Referred to as a "quintessential practitioner" for his work in Latin America and globally, Phil is not afraid to think outside the box and challenges others to do the same. Phil is a leadership coach as well as the author of *God's Relentless Pursuit: Discovering God's Heart for Humanity*.

For several years, Phil served on the Board of Directors of Vineyard USA as a Regional Leader, and until recently as the Senior Pastor of Pathway Vineyard Church, a multisite church based in Lewiston, Maine. Now, as the National Director of Vineyard USA, an association of over 565 churches nationwide, Phil brings intensity and a resolved passion for the well-being of leaders around the world.

To connect with Phil:

Facebook: www.facebook.com/philstroutvineyard

Twitter: @PhilStrout

Blog: philstrout.tumblr.com

Website: www.philstrout.com

JASON CHATRAW is an award-winning writer and author. He formerly served as the small groups pastor at the Atlanta Vineyard Church. Prior to that, he wrote for In Touch Ministries, serving as the assistant editor for Dr. Charles Stanley's monthly devotional magazine. Jason and his wife, Janel, live in Boise, Idaho, with their three children and attend the Boise Vineyard.

To connect with Jason:

Twitter: @JasonChatraw

Website: www.JasonChatraw.com